New Worlds in Old Books

Leona Rostenberg

&

Madeleine B. Stern

Other Works by the Authors

Books by Leona Rostenberg and Madeleine B. Stern

Bookman's Quintet: Five Catalogues about Books

Old & Rare: Forty Years in the Book Business

Between Boards: New Thoughts on Old Books

Quest Book — Guest Book: A Biblio-Folly

Connections: Our Selves — Our Books

Old Books in the Old World: Reminiscences of Book Buying Abroad

Old Books, Rare Friends: Two Literary Sleuths and Their Shared Passion

Books by Leona Rostenberg

English Publishers in the Graphic Arts 1599-1700

Literary, Political, Scientific, Religious & Legal Publishing, Printing & Bookselling in England, 1551-1700 (2 volumes)

The Minority Press & The English Crown: A Study in Repression 1558-1625

The Library of Robert Hooke: The Scientific Book Trade of Restoration England

Bibliately: The History of Books on Postage Stamps

Books by Madeleine B. Stern

We Are Taken

The Life of Margaret Fuller

Louisa May Alcott

Purple Passage: The Life of Mrs. Frank Leslie

Imprints on History: Book Publishers and American Frontiers

We the Women: Career Firsts of Nineteenth-Century America

So Much in a Lifetime: The Story of Dr. Isabel Barrows

Queen of Publishers' Row: Mrs. Frank Leslie

The Pantarch: A Biography of Stephen Pearl Andrews

Heads & Headlines: The Phrenological Fowlers

Books and Book People in Nineteenth-Century America

Antiquarian Bookselling in the United States: A History

Louisa May Alcott: From Blood & Thunder to Hearth & Home

Books Edited by Madeleine B. Stern

Women on the Move (4 volumes)

The Victoria Woodhull Reader

Behind a Mask: The Unknown Thrillers of Louisa May Alcott

Plots and Counterplots: More Unknown Thrillers of Louisa May Alcott

Publishers for Mass Entertainment in Nineteenth-Century America

A Phrenological Dictionary of Nineteenth-Century Americans

Critical Essays on Louisa May Alcott

A Modern Mephistopheles and Taming a Tartar by Louisa M. Alcott

Louisa May Alcott Unmasked: Collected Thrillers

Modern Magic

The Feminist Alcott: Stories of a Woman's Power

Books Co-Edited by Madeleine B. Stern

Selected Letters of Louisa May Alcott (with Joel Myerson and Daniel Shealy)

A Double Life: Newly Discovered Thrillers of Louisa May Alcott (with Myerson and Shealy)

The Journals of Louisa May Alcott (with Myerson and Shealy)

Louisa May Alcott: Selected Fiction (with Myerson and Shealy)

Freaks of Genius: Unknown Thrillers of Louisa May Alcott (with Shealy and Myerson)

From Jo March's Attic: Stories of Intrigue and Suspense (with Shealy)

New Worlds in Old Books

Leona Rostenberg

&

Madeleine B. Stern

Oak Knoll Press
New Castle, Delaware
1999

First Edition

Published by Oak Knoll Press
310 Delaware Street, New Castle, DE 19720 USA

ISBN: 1-884718-89-2

Copyright © 1999 by Leona Rostenberg and Madeleine B. Stern

Cover Design: J. von Hoelle & Michael Höhne
Typography: Michael Höhne Design
Illustrations: Office of Special Collections, The New York Public Library

Library of Congress Cataloging-in-Publication Data

Rostenberg, Leona.
New worlds in old books / Leona Rostenberg & Madeleine B. Stern.
p.   cm.
Includes bibliographical references and index.
ISBN 1-884718-89-2
1. Rostenberg, Leona. 2. Stern, Madeleine B., 1912–   3. Antiquarian booksellers—United States—Biography. 4. Book collectors—United States—Biography. I. Stern, Madeleine B., 1912–   . II. Title
Z473.R77R655   1999
381'.45002'092273—dc21   98-56395
                                                                      CIP

Printed in the United States of America by The Rose Printing Co. on 60# acid-free archival paper.

To the Survival of the Printed Book
In the Twenty-First Century

Acknowledgments

Since this book is based entirely upon the volumes we purchased, studied and sold over the years, we have none but ourselves to thank for it. We alone are responsible for its faults and for whatever merits it may possess.

Several others, however, have had an extremely helpful hand in its creation and development: George Fletcher, Chief of Special Collections, New York Public Library, and Jennifer Lee of the New York Public Library Rare Books Room expedited the production of its illustrations. Our gratitude to both of them as well as to the Astor, Lenox and Tilden Foundations, New York Public Library is enormous.

To Michael Höhne and Angela Werner of Michael Höhne Design, who lent their own special creativity to the book's typography and design, to Robert Fleck our publisher, and J. Lewis von Hoelle of Oak Knoll Press, who guided us skillfully through the various phases of publication. We thank all of them for their part in shaping *New Worlds in Old Books*.

New Worlds in Old Books

Contents

New Worlds in Old Books

Illustrations

Introduction:
Through Our Hands

A lthough this is the most bookish book we have ever written, it is also a personal memoir of sorts, a joint intellectual autobiography. Its source material consists entirely of the books that actually passed through our hands—the books we bought, studied, and sold over half a century. When asked what we deal in, one member of the trade responded, "Books nobody else deals in."

What were these books? They were the books that interested and intrigued us, the books we could not resist. They were not necessarily the five-digit books, the most beautiful books, the best bound books; they were not always the most important books. But for us they answered a need; they had a point of view; they connected with us; they often had modern and contemporary applications, and sometimes they prefigured what would follow. There were forerunners among them, stepping-stones to the future.

Very often they were little-known, neglected, and previously unstudied. We enjoyed the excitement of restoring them to a readership. With some exceptions, the giants are not among them. We never had a 42-line Bible or a Columbus Letter or a Chaucer first. We never had a First Folio of Shakespeare or a Harvey. We never had a *Sceptical Chemist* or an Eliot Bible. But we did have books that related to us and to our lives, books that tapped our education and understanding, books to which we could bring the fruits of whatever learning we had and that stimulated detection, books that confirmed our hopes and our beliefs. We had graphic eye-witness reports of events we had learned about in school; books that envisioned a united world and a utopian society; books that asserted the feminism we espoused, that confirmed the Hope of Israel we dreamed of; especially we had books that, in and between their alluring lines, restored the past and outlined a vision of the future.

Simon Schama has written that "in rare book and manuscript libraries lie the artifacts of our common memory; the documents by which we can reconstruct the life and culture of our ancestors, and by so doing understand our kinship with them." In the pages that follow we live again with volumes that connect us to the past and foreshadow the future. In these antiquarian books, all of which have been part of our lives, we have found worlds that were once visionary but today are actual, and we have found new worlds that are still dreams. These books, passing through our hands, have animated our thoughts and infused our spirits. Now we pass on to our readers these "artifacts of ...common memory," these new worlds in old books.

Here they will read about human blood transfusion reported in a letter of 1667 to a learned society that suppressed the account because it was so revolutionary. They will read too of inoculation against smallpox performed in 1718 by an old Turkish woman who "comes with a nut-shell full of the matter of the best sort of small-pox, and asks what veins you pleased to have open'd." They will read of dream analysis in the seventeenth century, not to mention one eighteenth-century pioneer who investigated the state of mind in sleep and helped give the couch of Sigmund Freud a long history. Even malpractice was anticipated in 1775 in a treatise entitled *Observations on the Abuse of Medicine*.

The remarkable technological progress of the twentieth century had its forerunners in these early books—from solar energy to thermo-ventilation, from a photoduplicating machine to a tunnel under the Thames. The past was at work, creating our present and our future. They even experimented with the idea of flight and interplanetary travel, these writers of the seventeenth and eighteenth centuries whose utopian dreams led them to envision a man on the moon.

On the planet Earth there were those who wrote, in those early centuries, of man's struggle against war and poverty, much as writers are still doing today. A social security package that included medical care, child care, and help for the aged was foreshadowed in the work of at least one eighteenth-century essayist.

The stark and stunning events that led to dreams of a better society are chronicled in the pages of our Eye-Witness Reports. Our continuing passion for on-the-spot ephemera is reflected in the graphic accounts of battles and sieges, murders and executions, coronations and nuptials that we assembled over the years and brought together here. From Lepanto and Spanish General Don John of Austria to the War of the Spanish Armada, from the fall of the Bastille to the struggle at Waterloo, great events were recorded in books and pamphlets by participants who rushed eagerly to their pens. Observers of plague and earthquake, fire and flood reported the suffering and devastation they had seen. Witnesses of the London Plague of 1665 wrote of the spread of the contagion along with the remedies of unicorn's horn and dried toads. Survivors of the Fire that followed collected affidavits on the origin of the "Dreadful Burning of the City of London."

The momentous occasions of the past are encapsulated here in these broadsides and pamphlets: the death of Mary of Scots, the execution of Charles I, the ceaseless work of a guillotine that decapitated, among so many others, a hapless queen—all are here. So too is a folding panorama depicting the coronation of young Victoria that we found in a bookshop in Tokyo. Although, as we know, "the search for truth cannot always be successful," these eye-witness reports bring us about as close to it as one can get. They enfold us in the past and make us eye-witnesses too.

The sufferings of the past have always led to dreams for the future, and perhaps the greatest of those dreams was, and continues to be, a utopia of united nations. As early as 1504 a Carthusian monk envisioned an international fraternity based on peaceful co-existence, and not very long after such a society found its setting in Thomas More's *Utopia,* the "golden book" that gave to the world an ideal commonwealth along with a "name that would abide forever." More's close friend Erasmus, in his *Querela Pacis,* reminded his readers that war had no justification and that, for a united society, peace was "the indispensable foundation stone." Despite these hopes of the early sixteenth century, there was no united society, no peace, no utopia.

Throughout the seventeenth century they strove for a union of nations—Grotius by means of international law, Sully with his "Grand Design" for federation. Utopians joined the political theorists, Bacon creating his *New Atlantis,* Campanella his *City of the Sun.* They seesawed with one another, the pragmatists and the dreamers, producing their ideal commonwealth that remained imaginary. "Perpetual peace" was the will-o-the-wisp sought by such thinkers as Saint-Pierre and Rousseau whose *Social Compact* planted seeds for the American Constitution. Immanuel Kant actually made perpetual peace seem possible in his *Zum ewigen Frieden,* and by the nineteenth and twentieth centuries "the literature of peace was probably as voluminous as the literature of war." It was represented by the work of the great humanitarian Jean-Henri Dunant, the great satirist George Bernard Shaw, and eventually by the Charter of the United Nations.

Have the dreams of all our political thinkers been achieved? Or are our United Nations still illusory and their Charter still utopian?

We were attracted to Americana because we are Americans, and we were attracted to its hidden appearances because we are addicts of research and detection. The excitement of discovering the unexplored, the untrodden, especially when it relates to a new land across the sea, is seldom equaled.

To find a life of Christopher Columbus printed in the margins of the Nineteenth Psalm in a polyglot psalter of 1516; to see in a Renaissance costume book portraits of Virginian and Floridian Indians; to read in an English civil war pamphlet of 1650 discussions of the herring trade with New England, not to mention tobacco and cotton spinning—are mind-expanding encounters with the unexpected. The American plantations had a way of popping up—to our great delight—in seventeenth-century Navigation Acts and speeches of Charles II.

The Anglo-Dutch War for mastery of the sea left a trail of hidden Americana in its wake. In August 1664, when the Dutch were ousted from New Netherlands by the British, New Amsterdam became New York and planted itself in strange pages: a French pamphlet of 1665; Articles of Peace between Charles II and the States of Holland; a 1668 *Description* of the British capture of New Amsterdam and the resulting birth of New York City. Nowhere in the titles of such works was there the slightest allusion to the American colonies. But in and between their lines we could feast on our Big Apple.

John Law and his financial scheme, the Mississippi Bubble, some-times materialized in a variety of eighteenth-century French historical compendiums, along with allusions to the American aspects of the Seven Years War. America was becoming a new frontier for the Old World, insinuating itself in the pages of antiquarian books and pamphlets.

In a sermon delivered in 1755 on *The Constituents of a Good Soldier*, we found the following pregnant remark: "Our Continent is like to become the Seat of War." The orator continued with a prophetic wish for "that heroic Youth Col. *Washington*, whom I cannot but hope Providence has hitherto preserved in so signal a manner, for some important service to his Country."

When Washington and the Revolution itself appear, unannounced so to speak, their appearances are dramatic and stirring. In a pamphlet by

Mirabeau we found a section on the mercenary Hessian troops in the War of Independence. In the columns of a French newspaper, the *Gazette de France,* we found details of Franklin's diplomacy in Paris, the American ferment over tea importation, the Declaration of Independence by the Continental Congress, and George Washington himself. Indeed, in an anonymous French pamphlet published at the outset of the French Revolution we found a printed letter from Washington to Lafayette in which the difference between the two revolutions was analyzed.

As the American colonies had inspired unanticipated sections in books on foreign history and economics, philosophy and political theory, now the United States became a point of unexpected reference. American riches in the form of furs from the "vast North American Wildernesses" were advertised on the printed wrappers of a pamphlet about a transatlantic steamship. The horror of American slavery was depicted in a panorama on the Great Industrial Exhibition of 1850 in London. There we found America's contribution to that event—a planter's armchair of "ebony" supported on slavery.

Once we acquired an account of an imaginary voyage to an island named Utopia located by its author in America. Whether utopian or devastated by the torments of slavery, America—especially hidden America—enriches the works in which it appears. To come upon the unexpected anywhere is a source of excitement. To come upon our country in antiquarian books and ephemera devoted primarily to other subjects is a bit like finding an oasis in the desert.

Reading between the lines may often be a prerequisite for unearthing hidden Americana. Suppression, prohibition and persecution seldom need detection. Censorship leaves clear and unmistakable traces. It is a sequel to almost every innovation or departure from the establishment.

Heresies of the sixteenth century—notably those of the dissident Luther—invoked excommunication along with censorship. The Papal Index was an expurging repository for authors such as Erasmus whose thought would endure, for writings such as the Talmud that would be perennial. While on the Continent all books attacking Catholicism were banned, in England it was the Catholics who suffered censorship at Anglican hands. The seesaw of persecution was at work.

The seesaw was particularly busy in France where, in 1685, the Edict of Nantes which in 1598 had given Huguenots freedom of worship, was revoked by the Sun-King Louis XIV. The Calas Affair of 1761 was also a French affair, involving a trumped-up charge against a Protestant, a perjured trial, and an infamous verdict. After the victim was broken on the wheel and burned to death, the Calas case became, in the hands of Voltaire, the Calas cause, and his *Treatise on Religious Toleration* led to exoneration for a victim falsely accused. "Through the medium of a book a step toward justice had been taken."

Meanwhile, England had contributed as infamously as France to the formalizing of censorship with its *Decree Of Starre-Chamber* of 1637 aiming to abolish a free press through oppressive regulations on the Stationers Company. The parliamentary revival in 1643 of the essence of the *Decree Of Starre-Chamber* would spur John Milton to write "the greatest of all pleas for freedom of the press," the *Areopagitica,* which states unequivocally that the killing of a good book is the killing of reason itself.

Just so, less than a century later, across the sea, the libel trial of the printer John Peter Zenger would result in an acquittal that became "the cornerstone of an American free press."

The newness has always been subject to condemnation. The pioneering great people the Index: Grotius, Descartes, Bacon. Helvetius' *De L'Esprit* was fodder for public burning. Rousseau's *Emile* was destined to be torn and burned. Paine's *Rights of Man* was tried for libel on the part of George III of England. The Revolutionary Tribunal of the French Revolution, espousing Liberty, Equality, and Fraternity, paradoxically practised censorship. All the condemnations, in the form of decrees, trial records, censures and arrets, are now rare antiquarian collectibles that have crossed our desks. The books they condemned are still very much in print, still proclaiming their once dissident doctrine.

Persecution and suppression were sometimes accomplished with the aid of the devil and his wiles. Jacopo Aconzio coined the phrase the "Stratagems of Satan" in 1565, and the sixteenth century was a particularly fertile time for the exercise of those stratagems which included "demonology and magic, witchcraft and sorcery, divination and prognostication." At the midcentury a French pamphleteer, Pierre Viret, tracked down the essence of the devil, distinguishing between white and black demons and analyzing the whole supernatural world. Sorcerers and their powers, witches and their conduct engaged the fascinated attention of Italian and French scholars pursuing the discipline of deviltry.

The best-known pact with the devil was probably the one formed by the sixteenth-century magician Faust, and the *History of the Damnable and Deserved Death of Dr. John Faustus* influenced a host of later writers from Goethe to Louisa May Alcott. By the end of the sixteenth century a failed attempt to assassinate Henry IV of France was traced to machinations in the "boutique de Satan."

By 1634 a sizable printed background existed for the pseudoscience of demonology. In that year—crucial in satanic history—Urbain Grandier of Loudun, who had been charged with demonic practices by Ursuline nuns, was burned alive for witchcraft. The case of the "Devils of Loudun" gave rise to a substantial literature, and, along with reports of sorcery, appeared studies of its eradication by means of exorcism and anti-Satanism.

With his *Daemonologia* the "wisest fool in Christendom," James I, contributed a major work in the denunciation of witchcraft. Another antidemonologist, Johann Wier, regarded witches as deranged—a perceptive diagnosis that foreshadows the thinking of Sigmund Freud. Wier was not only a pre-Freudian but a pre-feminist who found women, supposedly possessed by the devil, simply hysterical or melancholic.

Indeed, not one of the writers on Satan's stratagems who came to our notice was a woman. Women were rather either accusers of witchcraft, as in the case of the Devils of Loudun, or victims of it, as in the Salem witchcraft, examples of which we never owned. Our conclusion was perforce that women were less interested in the stratagems of Satan than in the precepts of Minerva.

Certainly that was and is true of us as our chapter on Feminism indicates.

The male glorifiers of women during the Renaissance, "whose vision of woman was somewhat less than realistic," tended to praise woman's role at home—not in the world. Even the supportive Spanish humanist Juan Luis Vives saw women "less as individuals than as daughters, wives and widows." Most Renaissance champions of women were macho males concerned with women in the nursery, the kitchen and the church. Ordinances and discourses, even papal decrees gave extensive advice on dress and ornaments, "painting, patching and powdering."

It was women themselves who asserted their abilities, expanded their roles, enunciated their egalitarianism, and—equally important—demonstrated their powers and talents. Vittoria Colonna, whose poems were prized by Michelangelo, was one; Gaspara Stampa, whose verses were reprinted in the eighteenth century, was another. "From the medieval nun Hroswitha of Gandersheim, author of six comedies, to Mary Wollstonecraft Shelley ... the literary shelves of every library in the world are filled with the outpourings of women."

From early on, numerous women followed the acceptable professions of writing and painting. Others, few in number but strong in determination, entered, or tried to enter, less traditional fields. In the eighteenth century Louise-Félicité Kéralio, scholar and author, also became a publisher; in 1840 Elizabeth Peabody opened a bookstore in Boston that became "one of the most unusual and influential in American history." Later in the century Emily Faithfull founded the Victoria Press whose employees were women.

The publishing trade may at one time have been non-traditional for women; the military profession still is. Yet Joan of Arc, the French Amazon Geneviève Prémoy, known as "Chevalier Baltazar," and Eon de Beaumont entered that profession with élan and panache, and provided material for fascinating narratives of the sixteenth, seventeenth, and eighteenth centuries. The concept of women in the military is part of the general concept of egalitarianism. No one voiced this better than the author—Judith Drake or possibly Mary Astell—who aimed in an *Essay In Defence of the Female Sex* of 1696 "to reduce the Sexes to a Level, and ... to raise Ours to an Equallity ... with the Men."

Woman's education, marriage and divorce occupied authors striving for the rights of women. "From the laws of inheritance to the right of suffrage, from a role as citizen to a role as office-holder, women and their male supporters ranged, pleading, orating, writing manifestoes." The French Revolutionary feminist Olympe de Gouges was eloquent in asserting women's emancipation and political rights. The American nineteenth century witnessed the strong *Appeals* of suffragists for elective franchise—notably the *Appeal* of 1871 signed by six distinguished feminists including Susan B. Anthony. Both Victoria Woodhull and Belva Lockwood went a giant step further, each actually accepting nomination for the Presidency of the United States.

The three women who, in our view, typify egalitarianism in all its aspects and highlight the feminist cause are: Mary Wollstonecraft, author of the first literary landmark in feminist history, the *Vindication of the Rights of Woman;* Helen Maria Williams, feminist witness to the changing phases of the French Revolution who lived the rights of women; and Margaret Fuller who not only lived woman's rights but wrote their clarion call, *Woman in the Nineteenth Century.*

Surely those three women brilliantly represent those "splendid coruscations of female genius" that shine in feminist history.

When Leona Rostenberg was a young feminist completing her graduate work in history at Columbia University, Prof. Austin P. Evans cautioned her: "Do not set your sights too high, Miss Rostenberg, since you are a woman and a Jew." That Leona Rostenberg and Madeleine Stern have always been eager to acquire books on Judaica needs no further explanation, although the explanation could be amplified by reference to the Holocaust of the twentieth century.

Though that Holocaust had no equal, the struggle between prosemitism and antisemitism runs antiphonally throughout Jewish history. The Christian Johann Reuchlin, who enriched Hebrew scholarship with the first important grammar of the language, was also an adversary of the antisemitic Pfefferkorn. Renaissance pioneers in the dissemination of Hebrew learning and language perforce served as champions of Judaism. Their adversaries were numerous and violent, including the Reformer Martin Luther as well as the Popes of Rome who charged the Jews with "mystical incantation, association with the devil, and the practice of usury." Through the centuries the "useless Jewish rabble" was accused of a variety of crimes, from coin-clipping to every municipal wrongdoing, and penalties included confinement to a ghetto or expulsion from their native country. Antisemitism survived and flourished culminating in the late nineteenth century in the Dreyfus Affair which was finally resolved by Emile Zola's vindication of Captain Dreyfus.

Prosemitism, the answer to antisemitism, was triggered by it. The French Revolution applied the Declaration of the Rights of Man to the Rights of Jews who found in Abbé Henri Grégoire a bold and brilliant defender. By 1791 the emancipation of French Jews was official, and "for the first time in the history of modern Europe" they were acknowledged equal citizens of their native country. The long struggle for Egalité was manifested in the long succession of pamphlets, petitions, manifestoes, and landmark decrees.

Meanwhile, the scholars, non-Jewish and Jewish, continued their efforts to investigate and expound Jewish history. Non-Jewish chroniclers elucidated the life of Queen Esther, the Mosaic Code, the ten tribes of Israelites. Jewish historians—Josephus, Kimhi, Abrabanel—gave us texts on rabbinical maxims, Jewish thought and philosophy, social customs, the Jewish Messiah.

The Messianic hope pervaded much of Jewish literature authored by Jews. "The Messianic hope is the golden thread that has gleamed through centuries of despair and desperation for many Jews, the vision too of a Jewish homeland in a regenerated world." Menasseh ben Israel, author of *The Hope of Israel,* represents that hope quintessentially. This seventeenth-century Jewish leader was basically a modern scholar. His most significant work, his *Spes Israelis (Hope of Israel),* issued in 1650 by the first Hebrew press in Amsterdam which he himself had founded, urged that Jews be readmitted to England, the country that had expelled them in 1290. In the eighteenth century, Moses Mendelssohn and Mirabeau became philosophical followers of Menasseh.

One of the strongest hopes of Israel was trumpeted in the pages of Theodore Herzl's *Iudenstaat* in 1896. This plea for a Jewish homeland was not realized till 1948, after the Holocaust had attempted to annihilate the Jewish population. Through the centuries, as our Judaic literature records, persecution has tilted with acceptance, Diaspora with Homeland, death with survival.

The history of the blacks differs radically from the history of other oppressed minorities. It involves "the slave trade, the importation of the enslaved into American colonies, the life of the slave in the West." It involves too the antislavery movement and its consequences. As our holdings testify, this history is unlike any other.

The tragic story of the black as slave has filled bookshelves. Its roots were explored between 1789 and 1790 in the British House of Commons where testimony of merchants and planters was taken on the life of the black slave from Africa to the West Indies. The statistics of slaves cover their capture and inhuman treatment aboard ship, the role played by manacles and fetters, the prices they fetched at auction. The *Code Noir* regulating commerce in slaves and their conduct in the American colonies, reflected their status as property to be bought and sold.

As antisemitism fought with prosemitism, anti-black literature see-sawed with antislavery and abolitionist literature. The Southern planter-poet William J. Grayson in *The Hireling and the Slave* found slavery the "best [system] for the Negro in this country."

We naturally preferred to accumulate more antislavery than proslavery writings, and our shelves boasted *The Negro Equaled by Few Whites* by Joseph Lavallée, the Abbé Grégoire's endorsement of the ability and rights of the blacks as well as his landmark work on the *Littérature Des Nègres*, and pamphlets on the St. Domingo Insurrection under Toussaint L'Ouverture that led to the abolition of slavery on the island.

We sought books that championed the intellectual egalitarianism of blacks and whites and books that demonstrated that egalitarianism, for example, Phillis Wheatley's *Poems on Various Subjects* published in London in 1773. Sold at auction at age 7, purchased and educated by John Wheatley, Phillis wrote verses that became not only a pioneer work in black history, but a clear indication of the equality of educated blacks and educated whites. The question, "Am I Not a Man and a Brother?" and "Am I Not a Woman and a Sister?" were being answered.

Demands for emancipation of the blacks followed antislavery attacks on the *Code Noir*. Even after the abolition of the slave trade, slavery had a long way to go. Thomas Clarkson, the eloquent English antislavery agitator, contributed to emancipation through his writings as the American Elijah Lovejoy, murdered in Alton, Illinois for defending his abolitionist press, did through his death. In 1839, two years after Lovejoy was killed, the American abolitionist Theodore Dwight Weld produced his *American Slavery As It Is*. Published by the American Anti-Slavery Society, it contained newspaper testimony of atrocities against slaves as well as the Grimké sisters' personal account of the horrendous treatment of women slaves. "Weld's book would provide a chief source for the little woman who, with *Uncle Tom's Cabin*, would help make a big war." Our biographies or autobiographies of former slaves such as Sojourner Truth threw light on the practice of slavery in a divided nation. Our Beadle dime book of 1865, *The New House That Jack Built*, pictured a Union built on civil rights. For us such bits and pieces provided insight into our national crime and our national retribution.

Many, though by no means all, of the writings featured in this book, graphically chronicling our Hidden Americana, our examples of Censorship, the annals of Feminism, the Jews, the Blacks, have come to us in first edition. First editions are especially interesting when they are also pictorial or conceptual firsts that mark ideological origins. The first likeness of the Reformer Martin Luther to be found in a book, the first book illustrations by Peter Paul Rubens, the first work on functional architecture in a particular area, the first atlas of America, the first appearance of the seal of the United States in any book, the first biography of a hero such as John Paul Jones, the first description of the buffalo—all these are luring to researchers in pursuit of beginnings. They were certainly luring to us.

So too were some of the great landmarks of thought and literature that we acquired from time to time. Our first pocket edition of Dante's *Terze Rime* published by Aldus Manutius of Venice still "breathes the spirit of the Renaissance" though it is a book for all time. Our *Rime* of Michelangelo that had its long delayed first printing in 1623; our genuine first of Cellini's *Vita* not published till 1728 are still invested with the freshness of beginnings. English editions of foreign works have their own special interest. We recall our English *Don Quixote*—the first complete English edition—published as late as 1652, and, jumping across the centuries, we recall our first English translation of Karl Marx's *Das Kapital* that "made available and intelligible to English readers the concept of a Marxist economy."

Since "much of cultural Europe came to America by way of books," first American editions may be even more appealing than first English. We think of a few that we have succeeded in tracking down: Godwin's *Political Justice* that in 1796 "gave food for thought to a people shaping themselves into a nation"; Montesquieu's classic *The Spirit of Laws*, the first study of comparative political theory, a work that influenced our Founding Fathers; Malthus on *Population*, a textbook for Americans who depended on European immigration; Johnson's *Dictionary* that "put words into the mouths of young America."

While many of our first editions brought their readers back to beginnings, there have been cases where reprints, reflecting the needs and demands of a later time, opened windows to the past and pointed parallels to the present. The fate of the Stuart monarch Charles I, executed in 1649, was reanimated for the French readership of 1792 as well as for their king Louis XVI, when Paris publishers reprinted contemporary documentary accounts of the earlier regicide.

Because of certain circumstances or additional references, some reprints actually add icing to the cake of the originals. Two perfect examples came into our happy possession. The first edition of William Wollaston's *Religion of Nature Delineated* is simply another philosophical disquisition arousing no great excitement. Its third edition, however, happened to be set in type by none other than Benjamin Franklin working as a young compositor in Palmer's Printing House in London. Who would hesitate about preferring the third to the first edition in this instance? The same holds for the second edition of Leopold Mozart's manual on violin playing, his *Gründliche Violinschule*. It was not till the second edition of that work was in preparation that the author added a prefatory note referring to the musical tour of his children. Since one of his children was Wolfgang Amadeus, the second edition of Papa's manual, containing the first reference in any book to his genius son, becomes an ardently desirable conceptual first.

First editions open doors to the beginnings of things; sometimes later editions do too. There is nothing cut-and-dried about books or book collecting. The only constant is their fascination.

One of those fascinations may be their typography or their typographical history. Uncommon printing presses and exotic types increase the excitement of books and add a dimension to their texts.

To propagate the Catholic faith in remote lands of the world, the Vatican in the early seventeenth century created its Congregatio Propagandae Fidei, and to implement its purpose organized a polyglot printing establishment. It specialized in the production of exotic alphabets, usually including in them a copy in exotic type of the Lord's Prayer or the Ten Commandments. What a seventeenth-century infidel may have found soul-stirring, a twentieth- or twenty-first-century collector would surely find fascinating.

Books printed by the blind along with embossed type for the blind provide other specimens of unusual and uncommon printing. An appropriate example of the former is Dr. Guillie's *Essai Sur L'Instruction des Aveugles*, "Imprimé" in 1817 "par les Aveugles." *Light For The Blind*, written in 1873 by William Moon who invented the first practical type for the blind, includes a plate depicting his embossed type for tactile "reading."

Printers themselves may be as uncommon as their typefaces. We mention four of them, each from a different century, who in a way led double lives. Our sixteenth-century example is the great Lyons printer Etienne Dolet who was also a humanist and freethinker and who, branded as a heretic, was executed in 1546. His seventeenth-century compatriot, Nicolas Catherinot, was an historian of provincial France and a printer-bookseller as well who specialized in the "libri brevi," or news sheets that he himself had written. In his dual career, one profession was made to serve the other. The great French Revolutionary, Jean-Paul Marat, was not only an important political activist but a printer whose imprint, "Imprimerie de Marat," signals the exciting presence of the "Ami du Peuple" who was assassinated by Charlotte Corday. No printer was more productive in two professions than Honoré de Balzac who enriched the nineteenth century with some 85 novels as well as with the output of an active printing press.

Experiments in type design often result in uncommon and exotic examples of printing: an unusually upright italic; the shaping of printed lines into what has come to be called "concrete" poetry; a title-page ornamented with a huge symbolic diamond to represent the brilliance of the Medici; delicate calligraphic typefaces; early color printing as in our copy of the mid-seventeenth-century *Bloody Court,* printed throughout in red to signify a bloody time. There is no doubt that printing, unusual or exotic, can tell its own story almost as clearly as a verbal text. For the collector of books, what more enticing lagniappe?

Without collectors there would be no libraries. As books become part of their possessors, possessors become part of their books. Tracing those possessors rewards the tracer, enriches the history of books, and makes the study of provenance an irresistible bibliophilic discipline.

In our pursuit of owners we began with the royals and semi-royals, not because they were the most important but because they were the most likely owners of bookish treasures. Henry VIII's copy of a volume of commentaries on Holy Writ enriched his library as it would ours, but probably had little effect upon the monarch. A book bound for the future Pope Sixtus V who would build the Vatican Library we felt noble enough to stand among royal possessions, and to represent later periods we included a volume of *Odes* that had belonged to Louis Philippe Duke of Orleans, father of Egalité, grandfather of Louis Philippe King of the French. A romantic novelette, its binding gilt-impressed with the arms of the Comte de Mirabeau, and a French almanac handsomely cased for Napoleon III rounded out our Burke's Peerage of books.

Two other books, minus fine bindings and indeed in shabby condition, we felt had a more royal provenance than any in regal libraries. The books had come from the collection of Franklin Delano Roosevelt and had been acquired by him during his youth. They were as democratic in appearance as their owner was in his philosophy. One was an annual for 1840, the other a French survey of the United States. They bore no gilt-impressed armorial bindings but they did bear the ownership inscriptions of our greatest twentieth-century President, and scattered in one were pressed leaves and flowers from his home in Hyde Park.

Literary ownerships interested us more than royal ownerships and told us more poignant stories. Browning's copy of the works of Paracelsus, a source for his first great poem *Paracelsus,* had been given the young poet by his father; just so Tennyson's copy of Petrarch had passed from father to son. When they stood on our shelves, they brought literature to life for us. In time they were joined by other distinguished literary provenances: Ruskin's copy of Tennyson; a dictionary of French authors with Chesterfield's bookplate and shelf mark; Carlyle's copy of the biography of the English commander James Wolfe who fell on the Plains of Abraham, with the owner's "Humilitate" bookplate; early Italian books once owned by two Italianate English poets, Swinburne and the pre-Raphaelite Dante Gabriel Rossetti.

The provenances of American books intrigued us always. Our copy of Stephen Sewall's *Hebrew Grammar,* designed in 1763 for his students at Harvard, had belonged to its author and included his annotations and emendations. Our *Star in the West* by Elias Boudinot, on the Ten Lost Tribes of Israel, found by Leona Rostenberg as a library discard on the shelves of the Columbia University Bookstore, had been presented by its author to Charles H. Wharton, who had been named President of Columbia College! We picked up a copy of Mathias' *Pursuits of Literature* and found it had been picked up in 1804 by a law clerk named Daniel Webster. We found inscribed in a book by Carlyle the poignant presentation, "J.R. Lowell from Maria Feby 22, 1842." Then we learned that

Maria White, described by the poet as "a glorious girl with the spirit eyes," married James Russell Lowell in 1844.

Women collectors of books are interesting enough to warrant an encyclopedia devoted to them. The libraries they form become an index to feminist learning. We think of the collection of the Comtesse de Verrue who died in 1736 after a violent and melodramatic life that may well have been assuaged by the books she assembled. The library of one of England's earliest and most distinguished collectors, Frances Mary Richardson Currer, was sold in 1862, a year after her death, and eventually provided us with a striking volume on the Reign of Terror. In this country, Estelle Doheny was a more recent and most notable woman collector of books. We were proud to acquire a volume from her library that must have stirred her own pride—a 1536 edition of Orosius that had been bound by a sixteenth-century English binder, John Reynes, who converted this work against the pagans into a work of art.

Some books require sleuthing to trace the connections of owners; some do not. Our set of *Poems* by Helen Maria Williams boasted a clear and noble lineage, going from one prestigious hand to another, from the Shakespeare editor Isaac Reed to the eminent collector Richard Heber to the distinguished bibliophile Thomas Phillipps. More detection was needed to identify the ownership of our Aldine Bembo of 1551 from a bookticket that read simply "Vigilantibus." The motto of the 3rd Earl of Gosford guided us back to an earlier owner, the great Aldine bibliographer Antoine Auguste Renouard. Holmesian technique traced the owner of a collection of Calvin's *Sermons* published in 1583 to a cell member of an underground radical separatist religious group. Tracking down provenances is only one of the many delights inherent in antiquarian books. All collectors, all owners of books, are of course merely temporary possessors. We too, spending most of our lives scouting for books and studying them, are simply part-time hosts of these carriers of the printed word.

It is salutary to remind ourselves that the books themselves— our temporary possessions—are invested with a permanence that we do not have. They can and will be passed on to future generations, even in the Age of Computerized Information Retrieval. Of the making of books there can be no end, nor of the excitements they engender. In 1510 the Strasbourg printer Mathias Schürer advised his readership: *LECTOR*

EME, LEGE, ET PROBABIS (Reader Buy, Read, and Esteem). The message still holds for the twenty-first century: READER BUY, READ, AND REJOICE.

I
"What's Past is Prologue"

Although he had little Latin and less Greek, he said it all before us. Actually he placed the nitty-gritty of it in the four words he assigned to Antonio in the comedy he called *The Tempest*. Shakespeare's "What's past is prologue" epitomizes the significance, not to mention the fascination, of antiquarian books. Written in all tongues—Latin or Greek, French or German, Italian or Spanish, Dutch or English—printed during the last five and a half centuries, bound in calf or vellum or morocco, or simply stitched as they came from the press—these sometimes crumbling volumes of the past are often the repositories of our present and perhaps of our future. At the end of the twentieth century, we turn their pages, we scan their lines, and, at some point or another, we gasp in amazement, for we have come upon a phrase or a chapter or even an entire disquisition that forecasts the future and sets us plumb in our own century or beyond. So much of it is there, hidden in these antiquarian texts where past is prologue to us, to our lives, to our thoughts, to our dreams and our inventions.

Even the idea basic to this book was anticipated over two centuries ago. In 1766, a French scholar named Louis Dutens wrote a lengthy two-volume essay entitled *Studies on the Origin of Discoveries Attributed to the Moderns!* And there he tells us that "modern"—that is, his contemporary—scientists, philosophers and technologists borrowed many of their ideas from the "ancients." Today, after devoting a half-century to scanning the books of the "ancients," we arrive at a similar conclusion. The books in which we have found the germs, the seeds, and sometimes even the prototypes of twentieth-century discoveries are the books that passed through our hands as antiquarian dealers. Doubtless there are a great many other books in which such origins could be traced. But these books we knew and studied, and in their brittle pages found a past that was also prologue.

In one way or another, we have all been more or less fixated on the human body, and so that seems a good starting point for our observations. The ills we suffer, the treatments we endure, the cures we rejoice in, all seem to have been endured, suffered and rejoiced in long before.

(489)   Numb. 27.

PHILOSOPHICAL
TRANSACTIONS.

For the Months of *July*, *August*, and *September*.
Munday, *Septem.* 1667.

The Contents.

An Advertiſement concerning the Invention of the Transfuſion of Bloud.

THE Author of theſe Papers returning now to his former Exerciſes, which by an extraordinary Accident he was neceſſitated to interrupt for ſome months laſt paſt, thought fit to compriſe the *Tranſactions* of all the Months omitted in one *Tract*: In the very beginning of which he muſt inform the *Reader*, that if himſelf had publiſhed that *Letter*, which came abroad in *July* laſt, *Concerning a new way of curing ſundry diſeaſes by Transfuſion of Bloud*, written to *Monſieur de Montmor*, &c. by *F. Denis Prof. of Philoſophy*, &c, he ſhould then have taken notice, as he doth now, of what

Ccc   is

How many books there have been in preceding centuries instructing in caring for children, from birth defects to breast-feeding, from the diseases of infancy to the training of children—surely enough to provide a background library for pediatricians. One of the more innovative is the *Paedotrophia,* a Latin poem published toward the end of the sixteenth century by the French scholar Sainte-Marthe, who offered his thoughts on the feeding and sleeping habits of children as well as their diseases. A century later, in 1698, the author's grandson translated his forebear's work into French prose, entitling it *The Manner of Nourishing Children at the Breast*—surely an early study favoring breast-feeding.

It is perhaps more remarkable that some of these early medical writers gave their attention to the human body at the other end of the scale and came up with productive thoughts on a science now called geriatrics. One of those pioneers was a French physician with offices in Grenoble and Lyons who in 1610 took time from his practice to write a book in Latin on illnesses of and cures for old people. As a result, he helped get the science of geriatrics on its way. Among the subjects he discussed were the causes of longevity and a regimen of life for the aged with recommendations for food and drink, baths and air. Among the diseases incident to old age Dr. Fougerolles singled out arthritis, catarrh, and the urinary disorder strangury. In 1610, apparently close attention was being paid to the elderly, at least in Dr. Fougerolles' office.

Arthritis had been on physicians' minds long before Dr. Fougerolles linked it with old age. As early as 1581 one Jeremias Seng wrote a disquisition on arthritis and gout, discussing seventy different problems concerned with those ailments and tracing his ideas back to Hippocrates and Galen. Over the centuries, another all too prevalent disease was smallpox. Most of us who still remember having been inoculated against smallpox as children recall that it was Dr. Edward Jenner who devised that vaccination toward the end of the eighteenth century. Most of us are not aware that his procedure had been anticipated decades earlier. The story is recorded in the *Letters* of the Georgian society leader Lady Mary Wortley Montagu, who accompanied her husband, the English ambassador, to Turkey. On April 1, 1718, she sent a letter from there to a friend, writing:

"The small-pox, so fatal and so general amongst us, is here entirely harmless, by the invention of engrafting. There is a set of old women, who make it their business to perform the operation, every autumn, the month of September, when the great heat is abated. … the old woman comes with a nut-shell full of the matter of the best sort of small-pox, and asks what veins you pleased to have open'd. She immediately rips open that you offer her, with a large needle … and puts into the vein, as much matter as can lie upon the head of her needle."

Upon her return to England, Lady Mary tried to convince the public of the efficacy of inoculation against smallpox and led the way to Dr. Jenner and the procedure that thwarted a dread disease.

Everybody was subject to smallpox. For other diseases, the working class was singled out—a situation that engrossed the attention of an Italian physician named Ramazzini who, at the beginning of the eighteenth century, before Lady Mary wrote her extraordinary letter from Constantinople, began investigating industrial ailments or occupational diseases. Having noted that particular disorders seemed to accompany particular trades, he pursued the ills of brickmaker and huntsman, soapboiler and tailor, blacksmith and hospital porter, pharmacist and tobacconist, and wrote the Latin text that became the foundation stone of occupational medicine.

While allergies also seem to attend every aspect of life, from breathing the air to drinking the water, the early "allergists" whose books passed through our hands concerned themselves primarily with allergies induced by clothing. They did not call them allergies, of course, but they did apprehend the fact that clothing had some relation to sickness and health. One of them, William Buchan, thought that fleecy hosiery might prove beneficial for asthma and gout, rheumatism and even deafness, and in *A Letter to the Patentee* published in 1790 he discussed the effectiveness of such apparel in skin diseases. A French colleague gave his attention to trousers worn on the eve of the Empire, while the English Walter Vaughan broadened the allergenic scope to include flannel and wool, calico and cotton, as well as boots, garters, stays and collars. The science of allergy was in the making.

So much of the present had its cues in the past. Human blood transfusion, a procedure that saves so many lives today, was performed for the first time in Paris in 1667 by a French physician Jean Baptiste Denis, who communicated his results to the *Philosophical Transactions* of the Royal Society of London. "A Letter Concerning a new way of curing sundry diseases by Transfusion of Blood" was printed in the July 22, 1667 issue, and describes human transfusion for the first time. That "Letter" was considered so revolutionary that the issue of the *Philosophical Transactions* in which it appeared was suppressed and another issue substituted for it. Nonetheless, the idea of blood transfusion was transfused across the centuries.

The surgical transplants that make headline news today were the subject of a Latin work by one Hermannus Grube published in 1674. Amazingly enough, he discusses the removal of tissue from a healthy part of the body and its insertion in another part where there is a lesion. He cites cases of successful transplants and details the methods of performing such operations. While there is no record of waiting lists for the procedure, the idea of surgical transplants is apparently centuries old.

It was not till the nineteenth century that an American army surgeon named William Beaumont wrote the first guide to the study of the physiology of digestion. The book he would call *Experiments and Observations on the Gastric Juice, and the Physiology of Digestion* was based upon actual evidence, since Beaumont was the first to study digestion in a living man. That living man was a Canadian half-breed who had been wounded in 1822 and been left with a small hole in his side. Through that hole Beaumont observed the working of the gastric juice and the physiology of digestion, and thanks to that hole he was able to produce the unimposing-looking volume published in Plattsburgh, New York, in 1833. One thousand copies of the first edition were issued. How many hundreds of thousands have profited from it since!

Beaumont is remembered and revered by scholars today, but most discoverers of the past have been forgotten. We think of the Dutch writer Marten Schoock whose treatise on butter of 1664 discussed the effect of milk products on disease and gave us hints of what we now call cholesterol. We think of another Dutchman, the sixteenth-century Adrianus De Jonghe, who wrote on the medical aspects of hair and the treatment of baldness. The teeth were a favorite subject for many writers, and one of them, "Surgeon Dentist to His Grace the Archbishop of Canterbury," enthusiastically dilated on "the exciting cause of dental caries." His book, *On the Loss of Teeth and Loose Teeth,* was issued in 1858 with a metamorphic plate showing a mouth before and after the introduction of a dental plate. The effects of narcotics were fascinatingly considered in the mid-nineteenth century—opium by the American physician Nathan Allen, hashish by a hashish addict Fitz Hugh Ludlow.

One of the most popular subjects for medical and health pioneers was what Dr. Nathan Allen called "the connection of mental philosophy with medicine," and what we now call psychiatry. Nearly all the pre-Freudians we have encountered gave their closest attention to dreams. The sixteenth-century writers, Ugoni, Giambelli, Pereira, interpreted their significance, investigated their sources, and divined occult portents from their nature. By the seventeenth century, our analysts were studying the influence of dreams upon character and health. Some were categorizing dreams of young and old, rich and poor, student and noble, lawyer and physician, saint and villain, while others associated dreams with the force of imagination and the role played by melancholy. One sagely observed that "though ... they be good ... they may so break in, as to make our sleep to be short." By the eighteenth century, at least one professor, the German scholar Herr Schulze, was investigating the state of the mind in sleep. The couch of Sigmund Freud had a very long history.

Not far behind medicine and psychoanalysis came the evil of malpractice, and that too raised its ugly head long before it flowered in the twentieth century. Thomas Withers, an English observer, wrote a book in 1775, *Observations on the Abuse of Medicine.* Medicine, he concluded, was abused by the neglect of useful remedies as well as by the pernicious use of unnecessary remedies. Among the latter he singled out blood-letting and emetics, purgatives and tonics, stimulants and sedatives. Had he practiced the law, he might well have led his readers into successful litigation. As it was, he thoughtfully anticipated an era when malpractice, malpractice insurance, and malpractice court cases would be part of the medical curriculum.

Early scientists as well as medicos looked and still look over the shoulders of today's practitioners. We pride ourselves on our achievements in food preservation, but have completely forgotten a calfbound volume of 1675 in which one Pierre Barra discusses the use of ice and snow for the purpose. Around the same time, a French writer aptly named Restaurand recommended the addition of iced wine to maintain the body's distribution of heat and cold. Earlier in the seventeenth century, the Danish Bartholinus gave his attention not to ice but to air, especially pestilential air, writing a dissertation entitled *De Aere Pestilenti.* In it he considered methods of cleansing the air by means of fire and fumigations, and may be said to have formed an Environmental Protection Agency on his own.

The nineteenth-century American chemist Ellen H. Richards, the first woman graduate of Massachusetts Institute of Technology, would have been happy to join the Bartholinus Agency. It was she who in 1882 applied protective methods to domestic life and wrote the revolutionary manual, *The Chemistry of Cooking and Cleaning.* For the science of controllable environment, Ellen Richards coined the word: Euthenics.

In 1814 William Charles Wells wrote his seminal *Essay on Dew,* a work that became the foundation stone of the modern science of ventilation. Wells' experiments started with a drop of dew which he concluded resulted from preceding cold. He went on to determine that the cold which produced dew was itself produced by heat radiation. Today, when we avoid humidity with air conditioners, we might give thought to the drop of dew that first captured the attention of Dr. William Charles Wells in 1814. It is interesting, too, that we once had a copy of his *Essay on Dew* in a later edition that belonged to our old friend the American physician Nathan Allen.

So much has been foreshadowed—even the abstruse science of relativity. Did Dr. Einstein ever read a French treatise by Scipion Du Pleix, *La Physiqve ov Science Natvrelle* published in Paris in 1603? Monsieur Du Pleix had much in common with the great twentieth-century mathematician. He too devoted his mind to such matters as time and space, infinity, the relation of time and motion, the unity and continuity of time and motion—all leading to the theory of relativity. Monsieur Du Pleix would have made an interesting colleague for Dr. Einstein at Princeton's Institute for Advanced Study.

The theories of science lead to the realities of technology, and from technology emerge inventions. How many inventions perfected in the twentieth century were conceived in earlier centuries and carefully described in books. Street lamps? See a *Mémoire* by an eighteenth-century French mechanical engineer, Bourgeois, who won not only a prize for his invention but the privilege of illuminating the streets of Paris with it. Transmission of solar energy? Read *A Description of A Patent Hot-House* (1803) by a Scottish agriculturist, James Anderson, who designed a hothouse that would operate by the sun's heat. Radiant heating and air conditioning? As early as 1777, before Wells' *Essay on Dew,* Adam Walker described his method of counteracting air pollution by filtering the air with a supply of "perpetual warm, or cool fresh air"—the birth of thermo-ventilation.

The much discussed Chunnel between France and England did not arise like Venus from the waves. It was preceded by the famous Thames Tunnel constructed by the celebrated inventor Sir Marc Isambard Brunel, and in 1840 a little manual, *An Explanation of the Works of the Tunnel under the Thames from Rotherhithe to Wapping,* outlined not only its history but the engineering techniques involved. Just so, an ephemeral French *Mémoire* issued in the mid-nineteenth century reminds us that our voting machines had their predecessors. In it the Parisian mechanic Alexandre Fichet describes his invention which guaranteed a secret ballot and reduced voting time to five minutes. A broadside printed in London in 1780 advertised the great-grandfather of our Xerox. James Woodmason's *Proposals for Receiving Subscriptions, for an Apparatus, By which Letters or other Writings may be copied at once* recalls perhaps the earliest attempt at a duplicating machine. Besides guaranteed to make a "small, handsome piece of furniture in a gentleman's study," it would make exact copies of letters, invoices, music and drawings. Even fraudulent use of such a machine was anticipated, and the apparatus, which sold for six guineas, was recommended for lawyer and diplomat, merchant and journalist. Twenty years later one Monsieur Hoyau developed a portable copying machine which he announced in an illustrated *Instruction.* The illustration strongly suggests a modern mimeograph machine, and the *Instruction* was issued by a woman printer who doubtless appreciated the advantages of a portable copier. The camera obscura was prologue to the camera, and in 1700 a student at Upsala, Haraldus Vallerius, presented a Latin dissertation on the subject, describing details of the apparatus, the lantern with convex lens and mirror, the darkened chamber.

Later in the century a French writer, Tiphaigne de la Roche, published a scientific fiction that anticipated most of the mechanical devices we enjoy today. In his novel *Giphantie* the author delineated not only photography and photographic development but the telephone and the telegraph, radio and television, and even dehydrated foods! In a little-known Italian book of 1629, *Compendio Di Varie Inventioni,* Annibale Salaroli listed many of those inventions: detectors of adulterations and navigable canals, medical panaceas and labor-saving devices—all designed "for the public good."

But it was yet another vision that stretched the imaginations of our early science fiction writers—the vision of flight and interplanetary travel. What the twentieth century accomplished, writers of earlier centuries foresaw and prefigured. Turning the pages of their books, we can indulge in aeronautical armchair travel, even to outer space.

Within the framework of a Utopian novel, *Le Philosophe sans Prétention,* the French scientist La Folie [no pun intended], having discussed the mysteries of electricity with Benjamin Franklin, presented to his readers "the first 'electrical' flying machine" in 1775. More than a century earlier, Bishop Francis Godwin, who was familiar with the Copernican system and equipped with a remarkable imagination, pictured his character Gonzales as seated in an aerial contraption propelled by birds. After a "chimerical voyage" Gonzales actually arrives in the world of the moon, and the book that recorded his journey was entitled *The Man in the Moon* when it was published in 1638.

Subsequent moon voyagers found far more than a man in the moon. Another bishop—John Wilkins, a founder of the Royal Society of London—discovered a world in the moon. In fact, he tried to prove that the moon was a habitable planet that could be reached by volitation. After his lunar landing he reported on the moon's mountains, valleys and plains, its vaporous air and its inhabitants. The celebrated French adventurer Cyrano de Bergerac also recounted an extraterrestrial moon voyage in an *Histoire Comiqve* that included "the states and empires of the moon." Still another moon voyage was the subject of Chapter XIV of a work published in Rome in 1728—*Les Avantures de Pomponius Chevalier Romain.* In this instance the voyager finds not merely a habitable planet, but a library, and devotes Chapter XIX to a catalogue of books in the library of the moon!

With such an intriguing destination as the moon to which to aspire, later writers proceeded to dilate on the techniques of aerial travel. In the mid-eighteenth-century, Ralph Morris wrote a *Narrative of the Life and astonishing Adventures Of John Daniel* in which the hero experiments with plane surfaces on the resistance of air and builds a machine actuated by a pump that enables him to fly. By the nineteenth century air flight was beginning to read less like science fiction than like science. Monsieur Landelle in the 1860s took all flight as his province, writing about balloons and parachutes, helicopters and aeroplanes, along with flying animals, gravitational problems, and scientific space explorations. By the time of the Siege of Paris in 1870, balloons (some of them occupied by carrier pigeons) were dispersing information and circulating newspapers with envelopes imprinted "Par Ballon Monté"—an early example of the airmail letter. One of those newspapers was a *Lettre-Journal* whose forty issues—a complete run—once passed through our trembling hands. By the last decade of the nineteenth century, Samuel Pierpont Langley, secretary of the Smithsonian Institution, could publish his *Experiments in Aerodynamics* with its mass of data proving the feasibility of rapid aerial locomotion. Armchair travelers and armchair readers were ready now to spread their wings.

For all the visionaries who looked to other worlds to conquer there were always more who looked to the world they inhabited. Concern with exposing evil conditions on planet earth and concern with correcting or improving those conditions run like strong parallel threads through books of the past.

During the 1570s, traveling in the French province of Berry, a French physician from the University of Paris was attacked by robbers who attempted to assassinate him. After his escape he told his story to a classical scholar, Jean Dorat who turned it into Latin verse. Dorat's *Monodia Tragica* appeared in Paris in 1576, dedicated to Henry III of France.

The gruesome details of a far more pernicious practice are disclosed in another sixteenth-century work. The *Sanctae Inqvisitionis Hispanicae Artes ... detectae* of 1567 is a manual for the professional inquisitor. It covers the means of detecting heretics, the role of witnesses, torture, and especially the refinements perfected by Spanish inquisitors. Such a manual could be surpassed only by shapers of the Hitler Holocaust.

As the inquisitor was anatomized so was the conqueror, along with the baneful effects of the wars he initiated. Two hundred years before Keynes, the philosophy of conquest was investigated, the devastation of nations that followed the conqueror. By 1797 in his *Histoire...des Crimes Commis Pendant La Révolution Française* the bold advocate of a free press, Louis-Marie Prudhomme, surveyed the atrocities committed during the French Revolution. Prudhomme provided his readers with lists of the victims, revelations of the factions and conspiracies, the crimes of the Parlement of Paris, the massacres and outrages committed at Avignon, Caen, Versailles, Orléans, Lyons—the burning of chateaux, the prisons, all the gory horrors masquerading as Liberty, Equality and Fraternity.

The French Revolution and its aftermath loved lists. The lists of works of art removed from Italy by Napoleon's armies make glamorous reading today. They contain the names of Raphael and Tintoretto, Titian and Correggio, although the jewel in the stolen crown is Leonardo da Vinci's La Gioconda. Mona Lisa, in fact, still smiles from the wall of the Grande Salle in the Musée du Louvre.

There is another list in an anonymous work issued a century later. That list includes the signers who met in London's Mansion House on February 1, 1882 to discuss Russian pogroms against the Jews. *The Persecution of the Israelites in Russia* records the speeches and resolutions made by Gladstone, Granville, Lord Nathaniel Rothschild and others as well as the Czar's refusal to hear petitions of the English Jews.

Writers who recorded and exposed man's inhumanity to man were joined by the legion who offered hope for a better world. The horrors of war led so many writers to seek the utopia of peace that we have given them an entire chapter later on. But there were others who gave themselves simpler goals to benefit mankind. As early as 1555 Hieronymus Osius produced a temperance tract elaborating on the influence of Bacchus and the effects of intoxication, and citing drunkenness as a cause of sedition and idolatry. Two decades later, Francesco I de Medici authorized a "bando" or law to keep the streets and highways of his Florence free of filth and threatening fines and imprisonment for offenders.

Scoffers at the law were early subject to police control. In England by the beginning of the nineteenth century it was estimated that there was one transgressor to every 22 citizens. The licensing of public houses and gin shops was linked with corruption; pawnbrokers were often in collusion with the police; the practices of "watermen, draymen, porters and hackney coachmen" needed supervision. So too, apparently, did the police themselves, and in 1803 one T. Colpitts saw fit to write *A Letter ... to the citizens of London ... Suggesting Improvements in the Police.*

Juvenile delinquency was increasing in England, as at least one *Report of the Committee for Investigating* that increase proved. Yet, centuries before, writers had been concerned with the role of minors in society. As early as 1557 a detailed treatise was published in Lyons *(De iure liberorum)* that considered not only such matters as parental authority and education, but what were actually acknowledged to be the rights of children.

Probably no subject gave more widespread concern among writers of books and pamphlets than poverty. One of the most interesting that we acquired was a 1580 study by a French physician and Parlement officer, Jean Martin, on work for the Paris poor. Martin gave himself a wide range, from almsgiving and charity to the responsibilities of the city bailiff and the treatment of the poor sick in hospitals. By the seventeenth century in England, *Some Proposals* were suggested *For the imploying of the Poor … And For the prevention of Begging.* The author, Thomas Firmin, started a workhouse in Little Britain for the employment of the poor in the manufacture of linen. His proposal has a familiar ring today: teaching trades to poor children. Firmin instructed his young employees in spinning flax and winding silk, stitching and making thread, and he advertised in 1678 that cloth made by the poor was available at the Three Kings in Lombard Street.

The poor and sometimes homeless sick were still with authors in the eighteenth century. And those authors concerned themselves with suggesting some form of social welfare in their behalf. The beginnings of what we now call social security are clearly discernible in their writings.

The great French physiocrat Dupont de Nemours, who would migrate to America where his son would found the Dupont empire, wrote his *Idées sur les Secours à donner aux Pauvres Malades* in 1786. There he outlined his thoughts on improving the condition of the poor sick by means of social welfare as well as charity. A few years later, Dupont's ideas were expanded by another French writer, Marsillac, who suggested replacing hospitals with civic societies and houses of industry. The former would supply health insurance; the latter occupational training.

Even earlier than Dupont and Marsillac, the French philanthropist Piarron de Chamousset had in 1757 in his *Vues d'un Citoyen* foreshadowed most of the societal advances of the twentieth century. Included in his social security package were communal homes with provisions for medical care, child care, care for the aged, and insurance with the ultimate aim of abolishing poverty. The twentieth century, still on its way to such millennial visions, hopes, in this instance, that the past will become prologue.

II
Eye-Witness Reports

*H*ow do we reconstruct a past that may or may not be prologue? How do we resurrect the fires and floods, the battles and plagues, the births and deaths, the murders and
executions, the coronations and celebrations, the pacts and assemblies
that preceded us. Surely it is from on-the-spot eye-witness reports of
events that later generations remember earlier ones: letters written and
saved; accounts in primitive newssheets; royal or parliamentary
announcements; especially printed records in the form of ephemeral
pamphlets read and thrown away, nailed to walls and blown away.
From the few that have survived—from the *Relations* and *Relatione,*
the *Beschreibungs* and *Mémoires,* the *Récits* and *Descriptions,* the
Discourses, the *Missives,* the *Accounts,* written often in great haste,
printed in small numbers, scanned and tossed aside—we touch the
fabric of our past. Here are the tales of kings and battles long ago; here
are the source materials that, taken almost at random from our
archives, make our history.

Vienna was besieged in 1529 when Turkish troops entered the city,
swept past St. Stephen's Cathedral, and were crushed in crossfire with
local and German defenders. One of those defenders wrote a free verse
narrative about the siege, published in Nuremberg the same year.
Christoph Zell's *Neues Lied ... Die gantz handlung des Türcken in Vngern
vnnd Osterreych* gives us an eye-witness account of what happened along
with a woodcut graphically depicting the Turkish encampment with
Vienna in the background.

Lepanto is a name almost as enduring in global memory as Vienna.
It summons up the glorious vision of Don John of Austria "going to the
war." And there in 1571 the Spanish fleet prepared for its own pending
combat against the Turks. When we read our anonymous *Relatione* of
July 15, we learn why the galleys of the Triple Alliance defeated the
Ottoman horde. We learn the number of Spanish galleys, the size of the
German and Italian contingent of mercenaries, the weight of their
ammunition, even the commissary supplies that included wine and sea
biscuits, hams and tuna fish. If we read carefully we can follow the

Spanish sailors of 1571 girding their loins and filling their bellies for confrontation with the enemy.

Only a short time later, in 1588, they prepared for a different enemy and another confrontation known as the War of the Spanish Armada. We know the colorful details of that conflict in large measure from the *Letters* and *Relations* that came out of England and Spain at the time. Lord Burghley, Elizabeth's great prime minister, kept a small army of spies to intercept Spanish and Catholic intrigue, and he was not above manipulating his findings to confuse the Spanish ambassador Bernardin Mendoza. In *The Copie Of A Letter Sent Ovt of England to Don …Mendoza,* he tried to dispel rumors of disunity in England, using a pseudonym to increase the confusion. During the same eventful year of 1588, an anonymous Spanish observer issued a *Relation* boasting of Spanish preparedness under Admiral Santa Cruz: the fleet, gathered at Lisbon in the spring; the able captains and crew; the bombardiers and armament. Both writers, despite exaggerations and distortions, disclose to us the intrigue on the eve of the Armada.

The English defeated the Spanish again off the coast of Cadiz in 1596 when the Spanish fleet, on its way to the American Indies, was intercepted by the Earl of Essex. After the surrender of Cadiz, Essex took time from his plunders to seize the library of Jerome Osorio which would shortly pass to the Bodleian. We know much about the siege of Cadiz from a contemporary German *Zeitung* printed in 1596 and sold by us nearly 400 years later to the Folger Shakespeare Library.

The wars of the past encompassed the sieges of the past. One siege after another punctuates our history. Between July 1627 and November 1628, the great Huguenot port of La Rochelle was besieged in its hopeless contest against the Catholics. Louis XIII of France appointed as official historian the diplomat and jurist Abel de Sainte-Marthe. At the time of the deliverance of La Rochelle, Sainte-Marthe set to work recording the details of royalist intervention and English involvement under the Duke of Buckingham, producing in his *Expeditio Rvpellana* an important and accurate source for this Huguenot struggle. Two decades later, another work, on the "last famous siege of the city" would be published. Despite the time lapse, this too was an eye-witness narrative, for it was the journal kept by Pierre Mervault, son of the Huguenot Master of Artillery during the siege, who had seen it as it happened.

Siege and deliverance, battle and truce, war and peace run like matching threads of scarlet and gold through the centuries. They come to life in the pages of our on-the-spot accounts. Possibly none of them was more copiously described than the fall of the Bastille. In 1789, the French journalist Jean-Louis Carra wrote the substantial *Mémoires Historiques et Authentiques sur le Bastille* in which he described the great prison-fortress where so many political prisoners were incarcerated. On July 14, 1789, that "bastion of tyranny" was besieged by a frenzied mob who freed the inmates and impelled the march of revolutionary events. The next year, the first anniversary of Bastille Day was celebrated by the federation of France at the Champ de Mars. Members of army, fleet and National Guard paraded before 300,000 spectators and were honored by king, queen, and the Marquis de Lafayette. Our pamphlet entitled *Confédération Nationale Du 14 Juillet 1790* was adorned with an engraved frontispiece depicting the fête and was accompanied with a medal presented to those in attendance.

By 1791 the glorious picture was tarnishing. As far abroad as Birmingham, England, the influence of the French Revolution and the destruction of the Bastille was being felt. We saw the effects clearly in a collection of aquatint *Views of the Ruins of the Principal Houses destroyed during the Riots at Birmingham.* Triggered by events in France, those anti-Revolution Church and King Riots of 1791 destroyed Fair Hill, the home of Joseph Priestley, which was sacked and burned with his laboratory and library. A once-contained revolution was increasing its force and spreading its influence.

The revolution that enunciated Liberty, Equality and Fraternity also created Napoleon Bonaparte, the observed of all on-the-spot observers. There must be few phases of his cataclysmic career that were not recorded in contemporary announcements, printed documents, memoirs and reports. We have bought, read, and sold a handful of them, most of them relating to his later years. In 1812 the titan invaded Russia as, in a later century, another global oppressor would do, and with the same results. In their retreat from Moscow Napoleon's soldiers aroused much rejoicing in other countries. As far away as Boston, Massachusetts, a festival was held to celebrate "the Russian Achievements over their French Invaders." Church solemnities in the Stone Chapel were followed by a festival at the Exchange on March 25, 1813, and a pamphlet was issued including names of guests as well as a transparency showing the

Russian eagle rising full-plumed from a Moscow in flames. The pamphlet commemorated the event, and in so doing passed it on to us.

In mid-June of 1815, Napoleon faced his Waterloo. From our copy of *The Battle of Waterloo* that battle could be refought. The volume is replete with documentary evidence, a list of the fallen heroes and their lives, and a large folding panorama with a guide to the battle. Also in our stock at one time was a *Description of the Field of Battle, and disposition of the Troops engaged in the Action ... near Waterloo.* This was actually a description of a panorama designed by an English panorama painter who visited the field directly after the engagement. His panorama, displayed in London's Leicester Square, showed the French line and troop deployments, and summoned up a living picture of a battle that has become a synonym for defeat.

Only days after that defeat, Napoleon Bonaparte announced his abdication as Emperor and promised a provisional government. In his place he named his son, the ill-fated King of Rome. Our copy of the abdication announcement was dated Paris, June 23, 1815. It was called *Dépêche Télégraphique* and was printed in the form of a folio broadside.

After Waterloo came an island in the South Atlantic named St. Helena. There Napoleon spent the remaining six years of his life. Thanks to the printed observations of eye-witnesses, we can spend those years at St. Helena with him. We can even join his voyage from Spithead to the island because it was carefully described by a fellow-passenger. The *Extraits De Lettres Ecrites Pendant La Traversée De Spithead A Sainte-Hélène* catches the fallen tyrant aboard ship—his mannerisms, his attire, his eating habits, his remarks and reminiscences, his indignation at his exile. A companion piece, *Documens Particuliers ... sur Napoléon Bonaparte,* written by Barry-Edward O'Meara, Napoleon's English surgeon aboard the *Bellerophon,* provides supplementary details of the historic voyage and its aftermath. Four years after the exiled Emperor's death, his physician on St. Helena, Francesco Antommarchi, wrote his *Mémoires...ou Les Derniers Momens de Napoléon.* Selected by Napoleon's family to serve as the exile's medical attendant, Antommarchi had arrived in 1819 at St. Helena where he proceeded to take notes not only on his patient's malady but on his modus vivendi. Antommarchi's signature was inscribed in the first volume of our copy of his *Mémoires,* memoirs that encapsulate the final years of the "little corporal" just as he was turning into a legend.

Coronations and fêtes recur in the history of monarchs as surely and as regularly as victories and defeats. They too are memorable because they have been recorded; otherwise we would be unfamiliar with the pageantry of the past—we are far more accustomed to its wars. Yet every century, even our own, has had its glorious moments. It was in the Court of the Bastille in 1518 that Francis I of France tendered a fête to honor the ambassadors of Henry VIII of England. They had come to conclude an alliance between the two countries, to be cemented—it was hoped—by a marriage contract between the French dauphin, then ten months of age, and an English princess nearly three years old, Mary Tudor. The facts that such a marriage would never be solemnized, that Mary Tudor would also be known as Bloody Mary, and that the dauphin would marry Catherine de Medici, did not interfere with the splendor of the moment. That was pictured in detail by an observer, a Milanese physician and poet named Bernardino Rincio. His Latin recital, *Sylua,* consists of 16 printed pages adorned with three coats of arms: those of England, France and Ireland. Our copy was fragile but it exuberantly conveyed the pomp and circumstance of a brilliant entertainment.

Another dazzling occasion over a century later lent itself to equally graphic treatment in half the space. An anonymous 8-page *Rélation* of 1660 is an on-the-spot account of the entrée of Louis XIV and the Spanish Infanta, Maria Teresa, into Paris on August 26th. The royal couple had arrived in the city to accept nuptial felicitations. The bride's baggage, we learn, had been carried by 2000 mules! As we read on in the brief pamphlet, we see the processions and ceremonies re-enacted; we watch the floats; we follow officers and musketeers, horse guards, pages and ambassadors, all in their flamboyant costumes and accoutrements, the brocades and velvets, the jewels and embroideries. We hear the trumpets blare, and finally we listen in the cathedral to the Te Deum. We too have been present at a grand fête.

Twenty-five years later, in another cathedral across the Channel, a coronation was recorded by the "rouge-dragon pursuivant in the College of Arms." Francis Sandford wrote the text of this grand folio volume describing and illustrating the enthronement of the "most mighty" sovereign James II in Westminster Abbey on April 23, 1685. The processions and regalia are enthusiastically noted, but of special interest is the rouge-dragon's mouth-watering description of the coronation banquet in the Abbey where 1445 dishes were served ranging from cockscombs and

A PROSPECT OF THE INSIDE OF WESTMINSTER HALL,

Shewing how the KING and QUEEN, with the NOBILITY and Others, did Sit at DINNER on the day of the CORONATION, 23. Apr. 1685.
With the manner of Serving up the First Course of His. Most to their Majesties Table.

Coronation Banquet of 1445 Dishes

fawns to stags' tongues and pistache cream. With such a volume we not only view the glory—we savor it!

In 8-page pamphlets or illustrated folio fête books the pageantry of earlier centuries is restored. One of the great occasions of the eighteenth century was surely the coronation of Catherine II as Empress of Russia in 1762. By then western civilization was impacting, if only superficially, upon an expanding Slavic domain, and that impact was reflected in Catherine's coronation. Our folio volume in German and Russian was adorned with a superb engraved folding plate representing the coronation chamber with statues of victory and a variety of insignia and regalia, all illuminated by delicate streams of background fireworks. A year later another fête book commemorated the first anniversary of Catherine's accession, this time in French and Russian. Our folio, published in St. Petersburg in 1763, was enriched with two folding plates of firework tableaux of the Isle of Pallas and the Isle de Minerve, their colonnades and amphitheatre, obelisk and statuary—allegorical fireworks of pageantry and celebration.

No nineteenth-century event lent itself more to pageantry than the coronation of Queen Victoria. Our stock has boasted two panoramas of that occasion. The first was a folding panorama in three tiers showing the line of procession on June 28th 1838 from Buckingham Palace to Westminster Abbey. We join the spectators, glance at the streets, the public buildings, the carriages, until Victoria and her entourage appear, and we are transported to one of the most significant events in English history. Our second panorama was acquired not in London but in Tokyo where we were attending an international conference of antiquarian booksellers. In between meetings we visited our colleagues' establishments. The clever Mitsuo Nitta had paid a preliminary journey to London, stocking up on works in English to offer his American customers. At his shop we found a folding panorama in color entitled *The Tableau of the Procession at the Coronation of Queen Victoria ... being An accurate Representation of that splendid Pageant.* Bound in its original gilt-stamped cloth, this panorama was twenty feet long and showed the entire line of march: the queen herself, the yeomen of the guard, the military staff, Victoria's household, huntsmen, watermen and bargemaster, life guards, trumpeters and mounted band, British lords and foreign dignitaries. We were part of the line of march on June 28, 1838. "It is 'subarashi,'" we shouted when we bought that panorama, airing our Japanese. It is still "subarashi"—wonderful—today.

So too are the narratives that chronicle the tragic moments of our history, events that stir not to rejoicing but to grief. Just as the coronations and joyous entrées have been memorialized by witnesses, so the dire moments have been observed and set in print—the assassinations and executions, the murders, the blood-and-thunder. Their records assume an immediacy that almost overwhelms.

We can be present at the scene of action and we can despair over its consequences, thanks to a contemporary Latin *Expositio* concerned with the death of Thomas More. The author of *Utopia* died—was executed—on July 6, 1535, on the order of his monarch Henry VIII. Shortly after the dastardly deed was accomplished, an observer sent a letter about it to Philippus Montanus who in his *Exposition on the Death of Thomas More* becomes not merely mourner but reporter.

Less tragic than melodramatic is an oration by Lionardo Salviati on the death of a Medici prince in 1562. The son of Cosimo I, Grand Duke of Tuscany—Garzia de Medici—died suddenly at Pisa, presumably from malaria. Actually, we learn from Signor Salviati, Garzia had killed his brother Giovanni during a hunting trip. Their enraged father proceeded to kill the killer by his own sword, yielding to murderous passion and creating a blood-and-thunder tale for sensation readers.

The death of Mary of Scots provided future readers with unforgettable narratives and dramas. At the time of her execution, ordered by her cousin the Protestant Virgin Queen, the deed prompted a variety of reports, defenses, apologies and attacks. The earliest relation of the death of Mary Queen of Scots by a Catholic was an anonymous work entitled *Mariæ Stvartæ Scotorvm Reginæ ... Svpplicivm & Mors.* Issued in 1587 when the execution occurred, it upholds the victim's innocence, dilates upon her preparations for death, and martyrizes her. Leafing through these brittle pages, we hear their twentieth-century echo, as Maxwell Anderson places in the mouth of his heroine the triumphant words that ring down the curtain of his play *Mary of Scots:* "And still I win."

There was no winning when, in 1610, the French monarch Henry IV, who had issued the Edict of Nantes that granted religious and political freedom to the Huguenots, was murdered by the assassin Ravaillac. We know exactly how the deed was perpetrated from a 1610 Italian account of Henry's funeral. Signor Vialardi not only included all the details in his text but enriched his relation with three remarkable engravings. The first was an equestrian portrait of Henry on his last ride; the second depicted his successor, the dauphin who became Louis XIII; and the third—a folding plate—actually showed Henry during the fatal attack. The background is enlivened with details of processions. The monarch, wearing his crown and reading a book, is shown seated in his carriage. Above him, almost in mid-air, the assassin leaps, plunging a knife into the back of Henry the Great, King of France and Navarre. Centuries before photography and yellow journalism, this text and its illustrations prefigure the assassinations that stain our history.

The texts and iconography of tragedy were repeated in 1649 when an English monarch, victim of tyrannicide, lost not only his crown but his head. The execution of Charles I, King of England, inspired a bevy of recitals and relations, several of which have passed through our hands. All published in 1649, they recount the final days of a monarch charged with high treason against the state and beheaded at Whitehall on January 30. They report the king's address and royal dignity, the demonstrations at the scene, the role of the regicides, the sympathy for his spouse Henriette-Marie, sister of Louis XIII, the actual beheading. Cromwell had called Charles Stuart a "man of blood." The bloody deed that ended his life runs like a scarlet thread through the books and pamphlets that flowed from the press at the mid-seventeenth century.

By the end of the next century a machine had been invented to facilitate such performances. Thanks to the inventor's humanitarian intentions, the guillotine rather than the axe was used to dispatch other victims of tyrannicide. Among them of course was the unfortunate Marie Antoinette who, after a speedy trial, was guillotined on October 16, 1793. Accounts of that execution proliferated and appeared from time to time on our shelves. An ephemeral decree we especially prized was issued prior to her guillotining—the decree that tolled her death knell. It was entitled *Décret de la Convention Nationale Du 3 Octobre 1793 ... Qui Ordonne le prompt Jugement de la veuve Capet au Tribunal révolutionnaire.* Here she is referred to, not as Marie Antoinette Queen of France, but simply—since her husband had preceded her to the block—as the Widow Capet.

Non-violent deaths evoke on-the-spot memorials too, especially when the departed are also the illustrious. The funeral of Michelangelo inspired accounts that have become sources for the great artist's life and work. With the aid of the art historian Vasari, Jacopo Giunti related the funeral solemnities for the divine Michelangelo in 1564 in the *Eseqvie Del Divino Michelagnolo Bvonarroti.* By order of Grand Duke Cosimo de Medici, the artist's remains were taken to Florence where they were interred in the Church of San Lorenzo with a pompous funeral arranged by the Guild of Painters, Sculptors and Architects. The honors paid the great artist, and the artistic passion of the citizens of Florence are reflected in this contemporary recital dated June 28, 1564. The funeral oration itself, delivered by the Florentine historian Benedetto Varchi, a friend of Michelangelo, was printed around the same time—another invaluable source for an incomparable life.

Cosimo himself followed the artist to his grave a decade later. On hand to deliver the funeral oration was a Provençal writer, Jean Baptiste Bellaud, who seems to have "specialized" in obsequies for the illustrious. His 1574 "oraison funèbre" for the Grand Duke of Tuscany was addressed to Catherine de Medici, and in its 22 pages offers not only the eulogy of Cosimo but colorful background touches about the Florentine Republic and the Medicis, the Duchy of Siena, the Guelphs and the Ghibellines.

Monsieur Bellaud was a busy man. Catherine de Medici's son, Charles IX of France, died the same year as Grand Duke Cosimo, and Bellaud was on hand for this occasion too, delivering a funeral oration that not only praised the dead but described his turbulent political and military career.

There are testifying witnesses not only for manmade turbulence but for the turbulence of nature: tempests, earthquakes, fires and floods. On August 7, 1546, when a violent electrical storm broke over areas of Belgium, Switzerland and Italy, a German observer reported it in a work he called *Beschreibung der grausamen erschröckenlichen geschicht vom Himel.* He did not neglect to picture the tremendous shafts of lightning, the deafening thunderbolts, the downpour of hailstones—and the results of that curse from above in loss of life and property.

Earthquakes also made popular subjects for surviving witnesses, many of whom remain anonymous. Relations of "tremblements de terre" at Lyons on May 20, 1578, at Malta on January 17, 1693 are only two of hundreds of earthquake records kept by writers who happened to be on the spot reporting details, devastation, deaths, and even the philosophical significance of such upheavals in classical times.

A few months after the flood of the Arno in 1968, we two visited Florence to buy books and pamphlets, some of which were not only dampstained but still damp. One of them was a *Provisione* by the Florentine health authorities issued in Florence in 1616 with the Medici arms on its title-page. It reported the flood of the Arno on June 30, 1616 and the measures taken for public health after the inundation.

Perhaps more interesting was another pamphlet about another flood occasioned in January 1607 by a tidal wave on the river Severn in England. In that anonymous *Discovrs Véritable* we read of the effects of the inundation in Somersetshire and Wales, the damage and the deaths. As we scan the 22 pages of this account we begin to wonder and connect. Had not *King Lear* been written in 1607, the year of the flood? Had not a "volcanic tempest" beaten down upon the old crazed sovereign? Had Shakespeare perhaps also read our 22-page pamphlet, and was this eye-witness testimony another unknown source for the tragedy of *Lear?*

Visitations of plague occurred almost as frequently as floods, taking their toll in all parts of Europe over the centuries, and accumulating in their wake a stream of reports. The course of a plague in Padua in 1576 was carefully traced by Alessandro Canobbio who, by the following year, produced an exhaustive survey in four parts covering symptoms, course and treatment, health measures and effects.

Probably no physical disaster has occasioned more on-the-spot treatises, accounts, and sermons than the great Plague and Fire of London. The Plague hit London in March 1665 and lasted through November. We know its medical aspects from the *Loimologia* of Nathaniel Hodges, an English physician who remained in the city throughout its course, although his history did not see print till 1671. In it he describes the patients who crowded his office, the spread of the contagion, the so-called remedies of unicorn's horn and dried toads, the poor he visited, the mass exodus from the city. We know the regulations issued by the government from a pamphlet, *Certain Necessary Directions as well for the Cure of the Plague as for Preventing the Infection.* Importation of foreign goods was banned; travel without a health certificate was prohibited; infected homes were to be closed; houses and streets were to be washed down; individuals were cautioned to search for marks of disease on their bodies; suggested medications included garlic, butter, and plague water. We described both these surveys as "contagious for bibliophiles."

The great London Plague of 1665 was followed by the great London Fire that burned from the second to the sixth of September 1666. Eye witnesses rushed to their pens; their reports abound. Affidavits were collected to supply *A True and Faithful Account of the Several Informations ... To Inquire into the late Dreadful Burning Of the City of London*—affidavits concerning its origin and spread. Individual experiences of the Fire were collected—testimony of scrivener and psychic, distiller and barrister, Papist and Protestant. In a poetic version of *The Conflagration of London* the English divine Simon Ford described the havoc of citizens, the use of pumps and buckets, the burning of churches, St. Paul's and the surrounding district inhabited by stationers—an area where the "labors of press and brain" were consigned to flame. The Fire had reached St. Paul's Churchyard by the 4th of September, consuming the books stored for safekeeping in St. Faith's crypt, turning the city of London into chaos "buried in its own Rubbish." The Dean of St. Paul's, William Sancroft, was moved to prepare a sermon called *Lex Ignea* which he preached before the king on October 10, 1666. When printed, the sermon bore on its title-page an engraved vignette of the Fire of London.

Dean Sancroft was deeply involved in the rebuilding of St. Paul's Churchyard. The rebuilding of the city also drew observers to their desks, and during the decade that followed the Fire, their observations of London's changed streets and alleys, lanes and mews, flowed from the press. So too did explanations of the cause of the Great Fire of London. Despite the fact that most of the writers had been on hand, their conclusions differed. The Jesuits were blamed by some, Popish recusants by others. The actual physical cause of the conflagration also evoked differing opinions from anonymous writers and from those as renowned as Samuel Pepys and John Evelyn. All of which is a reminder that even original sources of events witnessed by those who record them are not to be blindly trusted. The search for truth cannot always be successful. But in these on-the-spot accounts we come close to it. At battle and siege, celebration and execution, funeral and flood, fire and plague, we too are there.

III

United Nations and Utopias

Istory—so much of it graphically recorded by eye-witnesses—is also sometimes prophecy. At least that is what we two have discovered, leafing through our early books. The concept of our United Nations, designed and organized by so many scores of thinkers, we find was dreamed of long ago and far away. It is a concept both grandiose and feasible, and it is the ultimate goal of civilization.

St. Augustine located his *City of God* (which we had once in a 1483 incunable edition) in a church dominated by theologians; later writers gradually began to locate their "godlike" cities on earth, in federations of states. One such dreamer was a Carthusian monk named Ambrosius Alantsee. He hit upon the idea of what he called a *Fedus Christianum,* an international fraternity based simply on harmony and accord, on peaceful co-existence. His book was published in Augsburg in 1504, nearly four and a half centuries before the meeting in San Francisco that launched the United Nations.

It was not long after the publication of Alantsee's *Fedus Christianum* that a far greater work appeared from the press in Louvain. In 1516 the all but unfindable first edition of Thomas More's *Utopia* gave to the world not only the author's concept of an ideal commonwealth, but a name that would abide forever. His *De Optimo Reip. Statv* referred to the *insula Vtopia,* and *Utopia* derived from the Greek meaning *No Place.* The novel—for such it was—was described as a *libellus uere aureus.* It was indeed a *golden book,* this volume in which the vices of power and religious intolerance were annihilated and society had its setting in Utopia. We never owned the excessively rare first edition of More's masterpiece, but we did own a wondrous copy of the 1518 edition published in Basle by the distinguished firm of the author's friend Johann Froben. Its title-page had a woodcut border signed by Hans Holbein and it was embellished with a portrait of Thomas More and a plate of Utopia. We bought it in 1967 from our good friend Bob De Graaf whose business was located in his home in Nieuwkoop near Amsterdam, and we sold it the next year to Cornell. We know, therefore, that Utopia has been carried to Ithaca, New York, in an early manifestation. In all its manifestations it has permeated the centuries that followed.

HVGONIS GROTII
DE IVRE BELLI
AC PACIS
LIBRI TRES.

In quibus ius naturæ & Gentium : item iuris
publici præcipua explicantur.

PARISIIS,

Apud N ICOLAVM B VON, in via Iacobæa, fub fignis
S. Claudij, & Hominis Siluestris.

M. DC. XXV.

CVM PRIVILEGIO REGIS.

Foundation Stone of International Law

Another great book in the history of ideal societies was published around the same time as the *Utopia:* the *Querela Pacis* of More's close friend Desiderius Erasmus. We once had a copy of the Basle 1518 edition, and its title-page was also enriched with a woodcut border probably by Holbein. More important, the book carried the admonition that war was wholesale homicide, morally unjustifiable, and that peace—universal peace—was the indispensable foundation stone for a united society. Upon the tenets of More and Erasmus, in the early years of the sixteenth century, a United Nations might have come into being.

In the later years of the century, however, it showed no sign of materializing. Dreams of better worlds peppered the literature of the 1580s but a feasible Utopia was as remote as ever. Francesco Doni, a Florentine author, conceived several utopias in his *Mondi Celesti, Terrestri, Et Infernali,* but his most provocative remarks stemmed from his encounter with the infernal world—the seven hells to which Dante and Virgil escorted him. Doni was certainly influenced by More but not sufficiently to rise from fantasy and nightmare to reality. Around the same time that Doni was wandering between heaven and hell, a French historian, Gabriel Chapuis, wrote a disquisition describing the government of the world's kingdoms and republics. They were all there in his learned tome—France and Poland, England and the Swiss cantons, Turkey and Morocco, Venice and Naples—but by far the most fascinating of the countries was the one the author called the Republic of Utopia, an island whose people were surely presided over by the shade of Thomas More.

If most sixteenth-century publicists conjured up utopias, those of the seventeenth century grappled with ways and means of achieving utopian international accord. In place of dreams they began the production of nuts and bolts. The great Dutch jurist Hugo Grotius led the way.

Imprisoned for life for political dissidence, Grotius escaped with the help of his wife. Carried out of the fortress of Louvestein in the chest that usually carried his used books and dirty linen, Grotius eventually arrived in Paris where the first edition of *De Ivre Belli ac Pacis Libri Tres* rolled from the press in 1625. The copy we were fortunate enough to buy from a Brooklyn specialist in lawbooks had the irregular pagination caused by changes made by the author in the course of the printing. Bound in full gilt seventeenth-century calf, its message was a golden one for all centuries. The nuts and bolts devised by Hugo Grotius pertained to nothing less than international law which transcended the laws of the church. It was a natural consequence that, two years after its publication, the work was placed on the papal Index by Pope Urban VIII. We found a copy of the Decree prohibiting the printing of *On the Law of War and Peace* at a bookseller's shop beneath the arcades of Bologna.

It was actually in reply to Hugo Grotius' treatise *Mare Liberum* that the English lawyer John Selden wrote his *Mare Clausum.* Where Grotius had viewed the seas as open to all, Selden held that the crown of Britain ruled over the ocean surrounding Britain—a claim that failed in the test of time and served only to muddy the waters temporarily. Soon after Selden's *Mare Clausum,* the illustrious prime minister of France, Maximilien de Béthune, Duc de Sully, published his memoirs in two large folio volumes. Filled with thoughts on French economy and domestic prosperity, they found space for an early version of what Sully called his "Grand Dessein." Sully's "grand design" was nothing less than a plan for the unification of European states into a great federation of monarchies and republics. Control of the federation would be vested in sixty-six individuals elected triennially. The Sully *Memoirs* not only foreshadow the League of Nations, they form a collector's delight. In 1638 the two volumes were issued over a fictitious imprint by the author himself, who saw them through his own private press in the Château de Sully. The handsome title-pages are adorned with the hand-painted device of the House of Sully in green surmounted by a wreath in green and red.

Ideas filter slowly, but they filter. Proposals for international understanding punctuated the seventeenth century European press, and gradually new suggestions were added to the old. It became apparent to several serious thinkers that, in order to achieve a congress of European nations, it would be necessary to educate for peace and to develop a universal language. One such thinker was a Moravian pedagogue, Komensky, in his *Pansophiae Prodromvs;* another was the English scientist, John Wilkins, Bishop of Chester, who in his *Essay Towards a Real Character, And a Philosophical Language* announced that diversity of languages retarded scientific progress, and who outlined a plan to express ideas by symbols.

Despite the seventeenth century's emphasis upon pragmatic ways to arrive at international accord, dreamers were still visualizing utopias. Three such utopias are the *Mvndvs Alter et Idem* of Joseph Hall, Francis Bacon's *New Atlantis,* and Tommaso Campanella's *City of the Sun*—the first a satiric "discovery" of a new world, the second an ideal common-wealth, and the third a scientific utopia. This trio of worlds that are no worlds are illustrated with folding maps that trace utopian dimensions. They are also sometimes found bound together—a trinity in calf or vel-lum. Toward the end of the seventeenth century a student in political the-ory at the University of Upsala, Olaus Wernerson, wrote a dissertation that achieved print as *Luna Socialis*—a lunar society. What better loca-tion for utopia?

Eighteenth-century thinkers continued to seesaw between practical exercises in international understanding and utopian dreams. Frequently authors of fictional utopias grounded themselves in the lessons taught by pragmatists, and the pragmatists allowed themselves happy utopian inter-ludes. The century opened for us—on our shelves—with a new edition of a landmark description of an ideal commonwealth called *Oceana.*

Oceana had first been published in 1656 against a melodramatic background that involved seizure of the manuscript by Cromwell and its restoration by Cromwell's beneficent daughter. Now, in 1700, the free-thinker John Toland issued a new edition of Harrington's work, and the eighteenth century was introduced to a model commonwealth with a new constitution framed by one Olphaus Megaletor. Harrington's imag-inary constitution would have dramatic if not melodramatic conse-quences since it would exert considerable influence upon the introduc-tion of the ballot. His elaborate system of rotation and balloting was worked out in detail, and the *Oceana* would in time provide an ideolog-ical background for the American Revolution. Indeed the *Oceana* may have played a more vigorous role in eighteenth-century than in seven-teenth-century political thought.

Underlying every brave new world runs the concept—whether tacit or articulated—of peace. Warring nations cannot form internation-al unions. Especially in the wake of war comes the intensified search for peace. The League of Nations followed World War I and the Versailles Treaty. The United Nations followed World War II. Just so, after the Peace of Utrecht that ended the War of the Spanish Succession in 1713, the distinguished Abbé Saint-Pierre outlined his project for perpetual peace. Such a peace could be maintained only by an ideal government of sovereign states led by well-trained students of political science. Nearly half a century later, Jean-Jacques Rousseau elaborated brilliantly upon

A

TREATISE

ON THE

SOCIAL COMPACT;

OR

The PRINCIPLES of

POLITIC LAW.

By J. J. ROUSSEAU,

Citizen of GENEVA.

—————————— *Fœderis æquas*
Dicamus leges.　　　　Æneid. xi.

LONDON:

Printed for T. BECKET and P. A. DE HONDT,
in the Strand.　　　M DCC LXIV.

EN

Seeds of the American Constitution

Saint-Pierre's project, and went so far as to suggest a code of international law controlled by a Congress of Nations. This foreshadowing of the United Nations appeared in 1761 with a frontispiece engraved by Cochin, and almost immediately Rousseau's *Extrait du Projet de Paix Perpétuelle de ... Saint-Pierre* was issued in counterfeit editions. Our copy of the genuine first edition we sold two centuries after publication to Smith College. By then we had a United Nations, though international peace was still a will-o-the-wisp.

If inequalities engender war, equality is assuredly an ingredient of peace. Rousseau cogitated the nature of inequality among men when, in 1755, the Academy of Dijon set the question of inequality as a theme for investigation. His *Discours Sur L'Origine Et Les Fondemens De L'Inégalité Parmi Les Hommes* is, like his study of Saint-Pierre's project, a work of large proportions and traceable influence. In it he supports the belief that in primitive society inequality was non-existent, that property ownership was unjust and the seed of inequality, that mankind should return to the natural equality that was a birthright. Rousseau's ideas would filter through the minds of men who framed the American Constitution and invest the word *citizen* with fuller meaning for John Adams and his colleagues.

In 1762, the year after his critique of Saint-Pierre, Rousseau published his *Treatise on the Social Compact.* As Harrington gave to the western world the mechanics of the ballot and free elections, Rousseau provided some of the seeds of the American Constitution. The people, he held, were sovereign; they were the source of terrestrial authority. Government was their agent, and the principal criterion of sound legislation was the common good. Political theory had entered upon a kind of romantic period in which all things—including international peace and united nations—seemed possible.

A French pedagogue, Ange Goudar, writing after the mid-century, reiterated the hope for international peace but contented himself with a detailed plan for a twenty-year armistice. By the end of the century, Goudar's *Projet de Pacification Générale* was dramatically superseded by the work of a German thinker. Immanuel Kant's *Zum ewigen Frieden* was published in Königsberg in 1795. In it the concept of perpetual peace was raised above politics to the province of ethics and social conscience. In his landmark book, Kant envisioned a world where perpetual peace was truly possible. More important, many of his readers did too.

The ideas of eighteenth-century political thinkers did not go unnoticed by eighteenth-century political dreamers. Travelers on extraordinary voyages to utopian countries developed their own fabrics for society in which they wove the thoughts of great societal scholars along with their own visionary dreams. The result was a remarkable collection of eighteenth-century utopias.

The French writer Veiras, like Harrington, was a seventeenth-century man, but his *Histoire des Sévarambes* survived well into the eighteenth century. After an extraordinary imaginary voyage, his protagonist Captain Siden arrives at a utopian world "commonly called the Austral Land." Needless to say, its advanced civilization reflects the author's readings as well as his hopes, and the society of the Sévarambes is remarkably advanced in language and religion as well as in politics and manners. Our 1716 edition was enriched with frontispieces and copperplates that animated this "Austral Land." Another French Utopian, Tyssot de Patot, set his utopia not "down under" but in the farthest North—at the Arctic Pole, where he established his empire of rationalism and free thought. Utopia apparently could flourish not only in Thomas More's "no where," but anywhere.

The mid-eighteenth century seems to have inspired a flurry of utopias described by French novelists. All had intriguing names: the Kingdom of Mercury, the Frivolous Isle, the Isle of Reason, the land of the Cacouacs, the land of the Ajaoiens. Some were satiric in thrust, like Moreau's *Histoire des Cacouacs* that favored anarchical colonies where independence and liberty were enjoyed by all. Fontenelle's *Histoire des Ajaoiens* found space for a letter on the nudity of savages in the midst of a society of agnostics. Toward the end of the century, Beffroy de Regny, who called himself Cousin-Jacques, invented a lunar society that recalls the dissertation of the Swedish scholar Wernerson, and indited a Constitution de la Lune that incorporates Rousseau's concepts on equality, liberty, and the rights of man.

Even more intriguing than such a lunary empire is the far more earthly utopia painted by Louis Sébastien Mercier in his *L'An Deux Mille Quatre Cent Quarante*. First published in 1771, frequently reprinted during the last quarter of the century, and issued for the first time in America in 1795 as *Memoirs of the Year Two Thousand Five Hundred*, Mercier's novel marks a new departure in utopian fiction. Unlike the others, this romance is laid not in some remote, singularly named or imaginary locale, but in the future. Set in Paris in the year 2440, Mercier's utopia boasts not only the reforms in government, education, and society outlined by political thinkers, but a technological revolution. Here in this utopian future all sorts of new inventions were available to all citizens, from malleable glass to the phonograph and an optical cabinet with shifting scenes. Indeed the eighteenth-century author of this milestone in utopian fiction seems better prepared for the twenty-first century than for the nineteenth.

Judging from the books that appeared on our shelves, the nineteenth century seems to have been more concerned with a peaceful than a utopian society, and writers on peace were determined to implement their hopes. The Count de Paoli-Chagny, who moved to Germany to escape the French Revolution and subsequently vented his hostility in anti-Napoleonic works, wrote an important treatise published in Hamburg in 1818. His *Projet d'une Organisation Politique Pour L'Europe* is not only a plea for peace but a plan for a Federation of Europe. The Federation would be governed by a European Constitution and would boast European assemblies, European revenues, European ministers and diplomats.

Meanwhile, advocates of peaceful coexistence were not idle or silent in America. The American Peace Society, established in 1828, was dedicated to the abolition of war and the establishment of permanent peace. Its tenets were outlined in its Constitution, and at the time that Constitution was undergoing revision, it offered a prize for an essay on peace. In 1837 an anonymous author who called himself "A Friend of Peace" wrote a *Dissertation on the Subject of a Congress of Nations, for the adjustment of international disputes without recourse to arms,* and won the prize. In it the "Friend of Peace" stated unequivocally, "Whenever you declare war, you utter a deliberate falsehood... Whenever you march to the scene of action, you go to the work of *murder.*"

The literature of peace is probably almost as voluminous as the literature of war. Prize essays persisted in the purpose of promoting universal peace. William Jay, President of the American Peace Society, wrote his *War and Peace: the Evils of the First, and a Plan for Preserving the Last* in 1842. Jay believed that the gradual growth of public opinion against war would eventually eliminate war; he held too that an international tribunal should be established to arbitrate all disputes. His essay was both timely and timeless—in 1919, after World War I, it would be reprinted.

In England, the proceedings of the first universal peace convention, held in London in June 1843, were published by the Peace Society's Office and readers could find in them the concept of a league of nations.

Some of the proposals of the mid-nineteenth century were aimed only indirectly at peace and a union of nations. A folio broadside, for example—a French declaration of the Society of the Rights of Man issued in 1848—tacitly assumed that peace was among those rights. The broadside had no doubt once been posted on the gates of Paris, and eventually it came into our possession. Then, too, although his efforts were directed rather at civilizing warfare than at ending it, Jean-Henri Dunant surely was—if only by indirection—among the great supporters of universal peace. During the Crimean War between Turkey and Russia, the Battle of Solferino was fought in 1859. Dunant was an eyewitness of that struggle and, horrified at the sight of those left to die on the battlefield, proposed a plan to care for the wounded in wartime. His humanitarian treatise, *Un Souvenir de Solferino,* was privately printed in 1862 and would in time win the author the first Nobel Peace Prize. It would also help invoke the Geneva Convention which would result in the formation of the Red Cross. If warfare was still inevitable, it could at least be humanized.

The need for utopias had not yet vanished. Peace and international federation were still visionary. Writers could still dream of universal understanding. One of them, a French author Mettais, writing in 1865, set his dream in the year 5865 and transferred his utopia to Africa. Another, the American Joaquin Miller writing in 1893, produced in his *The Building of the City Beautiful* a utopian romance that crusaded for brotherly love and goodwill toward men in a perfect state where the absence of money was coupled with labor for all, where human resources were as free as thought and conduct.

The firm of Rostenberg and Stern does not often deal in twentieth-century books. Through the years we have advanced from the sixteenth century to 1800 and even beyond, but we balk at our own extraordinary century, at once the worst and the best of the centuries preceding. But we have handled two twentieth-century works that must conclude this chapter. The first was written with tongue in cheek by the great George Bernard Shaw. It was published in London in 1929 by the Fabian Tract Society, and it was entitled *The League of Nations.* Shaw described the League as "a school for the new international statesmanship as against the old Foreign Office diplomacy," and wrote as if he did not quite believe the League's authority to prevent war. As usual, G.B.S. was right.

Then too we once had in our stock a copy of the *Charter of the United Nations.* It was issued as No. 622 of an edition limited to 1000 copies, and it was signed by the typographer. Other signatures—those of leading members of the delegations—were in facsimile. The Charter, signed at San Francisco in 1945, included articles on the purposes and ideals of the United Nations, the peaceful settlement of disputes, the principle of international cooperation. It is all there—the strivings of centuries, the utopian dreams. And it exists. We think of that lunary empire that enchanted a few of our utopian writers, and we think too that we have actually visited the moon.

We put the two thoughts together. We have landed on the moon, and the United Nations exists. We have realized the concept of a peaceful federation of nations, and we have visited the lunary empire. Or have we? How close are we to the plans and proposals, the outlines and dreams of the authors of the last five centuries? Have we realized them, or are we still dreaming utopian dreams?

IV
Hidden Americana

The sixteenth century was blessed in its possession of a comparatively new technology to use, and a comparatively new world to explore. A country beyond the seas had been discovered, and to describe it printing by movable type was available. As a result, America would add a new dimension to the mind's map. Four centuries later, we who deal in books scan sixteenth-century pages to search for the beginnings of our country. The search for anything that has not been found before is the lure that draws all explorers and researchers. To those who live with books there is no greater excitement than the discovery in their pages of the unexplored, the untrodden, the new. The sixteenth-century writer, alive with the knowledge that a new land had been found across the sea, sometimes took occasion to mention it when he wrote on history or geography, on politics or theology, or even on clothing. Such books may carry no reference whatever to the western world on their title-pages. Allusions to it are often tucked modestly between the lines, and when discovered four centuries later, become eye-openers, mind-expanders. Today, when we research those books, we become not only explorers but discoverers.

In 1516 a handsome polyglot psalter was published in Genoa. The editor of this folio volume that supplied the text of David's psalms in Hebrew and Arabic, Greek and Latin, printed it at his own expense. He was Agostino Giustiniani, born in Genoa, a student of languages who was the first to teach Hebrew in the University of Paris. When he died in 1536 he would leave his library to his native city.*

Giustiniani left another legacy too, and students leafing through his polyglot psalter could share it. When they came to the text of Psalm XIX, reading, "The heavens declare the glory of God; and the firmament sheweth his handywork," they would gasp in amazement. Set in type around the nineteenth psalm of David was the story of a Genoese citizen named Christopher Columbus who had discovered an unknown conti-

---

*This psalter and a few other items in this chapter are discussed from another point of view in Rostenberg-Stern, *Connections: Our Selves—Our Books* (Santa Monica 1994).

HABITI ANTICHI,
ET MODERNI
di tutto il Mondo.

DI CESARE VECELLIO.

Di nuouo accresciuti di molte figure.

VESTITVS
Antiquorum, recentiorumque
totius Orbis.

PER SVLSTATIVM
Gratilianum Senapolensis
Latinè declarati.

IN VENETIA,
Appresso i Sessa.

Costumes of 1598

nent. Here unexpectedly, thrillingly, appeared the first account in any book of Columbus' life. Born, as Columbus had been, in Genoa, overwhelmed by the tales of his discoveries, Giustiniani had bordered the nineteenth psalm with this record of navigation and penetration into unknown territories and unexplored islands, the natives and their customs, the flora, the Fortunate Isles. In this landmark marginal printing, published only ten years after the discoverer's death, the heavens indeed declared the glory of God.

Our copy of this magnificent hidden Americanum was enriched by its provenance. Long before it passed to the Chatsworth Library, it had been owned by the sixteenth-century classical scholar Isaac Casaubon, a Calvinist who had sought refuge in England and become a confidant of James I. At the time of the Columbus Quincentenary, a great American library acquired our polyglot psalter weighted with its nugget of gold from the New World.

Giustiniani was also the author of the *Annals* of the Republic of Genoa, and there too he found space to refer to the Columbus voyages. Not much space. Seldom was more than a page or two devoted to the Genoese citizen Columbus and the "Nuovo Mondo" he had discovered in the sixteenth-century compendiums about Genoa. Uberto Foglietta included a sketch of the voyager among the city-state's distinguished, but only a sketch. As Columbus was mentioned *en passant,* so the New World itself was merely a footnote in the geographies of the Renaissance. Henricus Loritus in his *De Geographia Liber unus,* for example, elaborated copiously on the lands of Europe, Africa and Asia, mentioning briefly on one page the western land called America—the islands of "Spagnola & Isabella," and the navigations of Columbus and Amerigo Vespucci.

During the Renaissance America occasionally appeared as a modest insertion in volumes on a variety of subjects. Luca Contile in his compilation of emblems representing members of the Academy of the Affidati and others, included 115 copper-engraved illustrations along with a map that showed the continent of America. Toward the end of the century, a French writer, Antoine Arnauld, blaming Philip II of Spain for all the troubles in France, referred incidentally in his *Anti-Espagnol* to Spanish conquests in Peru, where the Spaniards exploited thousands in the mines and subjected the natives to excessive cruelties.

A distinguished and eagerly sought work on Renaissance costume by the Italian artist Cesare Vecelli is adorned with over 500 plates showing the *Habiti Antichi, Et Moderni di tutto il Mondo*—the costumes of all the world. Italian and Russian, English and French, Turkish and Moslem attires are depicted. And in this remarkable costume book the artist took occasion to include Peruvians and Mexicans, Virginian and Floridian Indians. Interestingly enough, those American costumes do not appear in the first edition of Vecelli's book. It was not until the century had almost ended that the artist added his American portraits.

By the seventeenth century, the western world was becoming a bit more than a footnote, although it still often appeared as Hidden Americana, unannounced in title-pages. The hidden Americana that crossed our desk and bore our scrutiny included seventeenth-century éloges of eminent literary, political and theological leaders such as a compilation by Jacopo Gaddi that offered short accounts of Amerigo Vespucci and the naming of the "new world of America." We found that the American tribes were still regarded as the "American barbarians" in a demographic study by the German Christopher Besold, and in a discussion of cosmographical and astronomical problems by the Italian scientist Micalori we hit upon passing references to the division of the New World between Spain and Portugal.

To mid-seventeenth-century writers of hidden Americana, however, the advantages to be accrued from dividing up that New World were becoming increasingly clear. In 1988 we purchased from a London firm a large collection of seventeenth-century English pamphlets centering about Cromwell and the civil war. When they arrived we studied them avidly, and as we studied them we scanned one that alarmingly increased our pulse rates. It was a brief study entitled *A Diamond or Rich Jewel, Presented to the Common-wealth of England, for the use of all Marchants and Tradesmen.* A rich jewel, indeed. Published in London in 1650, the pamphlet was written by a self-styled "Captain" from Devon, Samuel Chappel, who served in the Parliament during the 1640s, was a merchant, and was imprisoned for debt. "Captain" Chappel had experienced the trials of poverty and had lived through the economic deterioration of the English civil war. What better way to enrich his country—and perhaps himself—than by trade with America? In the thirty pages of his *Diamond or Rich Jewel* Chappel discusses the herring trade with New England, shipping, tobacco, cotton spinning—exploitation of the riches of the new world for the benefit of the old. For a writer in prison for debt, what more enticing windfall to dream of? We mined that pamphlet for the treasure suggested in its title, and found it—not in the form of gold and silver, but of herring and tobacco from Hidden Americana. This "diamond or rich jewel" had been presented, we thought, less to the Commonwealth of England than to two American booksellers.

Both tobacco and herring continued to captivate foreign writers who did not bother to mention America in their titles. In his *Discovrs dv Tabac* the French physician Edmé Baillard wrote a eulogy of tobacco discussing the American sources of the plant, its role as an American cult, its importation abroad, Drake's introduction of tobacco to England, tobacco even in Antarctica, and—irony of ironies—the medicinal uses of tobacco. Our copy of the first edition of this work published in 1668 included three delicate woodcuts of the tobacco plant.

As for herring, that fish was the subject of *An Act Giving License for Transporting Fish in Forreign Bottoms,* concerned with the herring fleet. Its Americana interest was revealed in the startling statement that "It may be lawful for every person ... to Buy and Transport out of Newfound-land, or New-England or any of the Parts thereof, any sorts of Fish whatsoever, without paying any Custom, or other duty for the Same." Much of Europe was apparently fishing for American herring.

That *Act* on the herring fleet bore on its title-page the arms of the Commonwealth of England. It had been issued in 1657 by the government of Oliver Cromwell. When Charles II was restored to the throne of England in 1660 he showed an interest similar to Cromwell's in cornering the American market. He re-enacted the Navigation Act of 1651, ordaining that "No goods are to be imported from the Plantations but in English ships. ... No Sugars, Tobacco, Cotton-Wooll ... of the Growth, Production or Manufacture of any English Plantations in America ..." Shortly after his restoration, Charles II delivered a speech before Parliament published along with the speech of the Lord Chancellor, Edward Hyde, Lord Clarendon. Lord Clarendon did not fail to mention the welfare of the American colonies in a pregnant sentence: "The King... [is] very solicitous for the improvement and prosperity of His Plantations abroad, where there is such large room for the Industry and Reception of such who shall desire to go thither."

The colonial and trade disputes between England and Holland came to a head in the fall of 1663, culminating in the Anglo-Dutch War for mastery of the sea. In August 1664 the British ousted the Dutch from New Netherlands, and its town, New Amsterdam, became New York. For us as American booksellers, any hidden Americanum arouses delight. For us as New York natives, any hidden reference to our city inspires ecstasy. Upon at least four different occasions we have found in and between the lines of seventeenth-century ephemeral works that make no mention of America or of New Netherlands in their titles, thrilling references to our Big Apple.

One of them we found in a French dealer's shop on the rue de l'Echaudé, a narrow cobbled lane on Paris' Left Bank. A collection of 22 seventeenth-century French pamphlets offered for sale tempted us, and was duly purchased. When we returned home and examined our selections we saw that the collection included one item entitled *Diverses Pièces Servans de Réponse Avx Discovrs Pvbliez Par Les Hollandois, svr ce qvi s'est passé entre l'Angleterre et La Hollande*. Its date was 1665. What had passed between England and Holland was, of course, the Anglo-Dutch War, the struggle that resulted in the Dutch loss of New Amsterdam. Here was the account in an extremely rare French edition—and before long it passed from us to precisely where it belonged, the shelves of the New York Historical Society.

In the Peace of Breda, July 31, 1667, Holland ceded New Netherland to the English. Appropriately, from a Dutch bookseller in 1969, just after the tercentenary of the Treaty, we bought its all-important *Articuli Pacis* between Charles II of England and the States of Holland. The arms of the United Provinces were on the title-page, but only on the title-page. They would be erased from New Netherland and its capital city, New Amsterdam. We had purchased what we called a "foundation piece for the future development of 'fun city'!"

More recently we acquired an illustrated quarto *Déscription Exacte De tout ce qui s'est passé dans les Guerres Entre le Roy d'Angleterre ... [et] les Estats des Provinces Unies du Pays-Bas*. Published in 1668, this French translation from the Dutch covered the period from 1664 to the Peace of Breda of 1667, and so included a contemporary report of the British capture of New Amsterdam from the Netherlands and the consequent birth of New York City. It also included an illustrated account of the great Fire of London that burned in 1666. Was the former any compensation for the latter?

In 1673 New York was briefly recaptured by the Dutch vice-admiral Evertsen. In an agreement signed in December of that year, the Dutch consented to return the colony to the English. In 1989 we purchased an unprepossessing-looking bit of ephemera published at The Hague in 1673: *A Letter From The States-General of the United Provinces of the Low Countries to the King of Great Britain.* The *Letter* was the agreement by which the colony was restored to the British.

The seventeenth century restored to us not only our New York but several fascinating pieces of Hidden Americana. One was an extraordinary forecast of things to be. A curious relation, ascribed to Henry Neville, concerned the Isle of Pines, "Situata oltre la linea Equinotiale" in Cuba. We found it in an extremely rare Italian version. According to the author, the island had first been explored in 1589 by one man and four women who had been shipwrecked on an English vessel. By the time the relation appeared, some seventy-five years later, the original inhabitants had propagated more than 11,000 individuals! The New World had come a long way in less than a century—not only qualitatively but quantitatively.

By the 1700s the American continent was appearing not merely marginally in a psalter or parenthetically in a geography, but in more substantial references, even in our Hidden Americana. When His Catholic Majesty, Philip V of Spain, issued a *Manifesto* in 1739 occasioned by the signing of a Convention with England, numerous allusions were made to America—its plantations and forts, the Assiento Company for providing slaves, especially navigation and trade in the West Indies and North America. Trade with America intensified, heightening European interest in a continent that was becoming a new frontier for an old world. In a fascinating hidden Americanum entitled *L'Angleterre Sacrifiée A L'Electorat De Hannovre*—ostensibly a complaint regarding English subservience to the House of Hanover—there are all sorts of American references: Spain and contraband commerce in America; British defense in America; even the statement that "our last conquest in America has turned our head." How far French heads were turned in regard to America was evidenced in the work of Charles Pinot Duclos, *Mémoires Secrets sur les Règnes De Louis XIV Et De Louis XV.* In that compendium there were discussions of John Law and the Mississippi Bubble, the role of the Indians, and even the Jesuits in America.

It was natural that the Seven Years War should have its American counterpart: the French and Indian War. In a detailed analysis of the Seven Years War—*Histoire de la Dernière Guerre*—therefore, we have found copious allusions to events across the seas. The fall of Quebec, the English capture of Cuba, references to the Mississippi River are all here in a work that makes clear that the new world was now essentially English. The same message is conveyed in Choiseul-Stainville's *Mémoire Historique sur la Négociation de la France & de l'Angleterre.* Although America is absent from the title-page, the date of 1761 alerts the researcher to the fact that at that time Franco-English negotiations would have to concern the colonial world of North America. A similar story is told in our copy of *Preliminary Articles of Peace between His Britannick Majesty, and the Most Christian King, and the Catholick King* published in London in 1762 with text in double columns of English and French. The treaty would grant to England all the French territory east of the Mississippi except for New Orleans, although France was granted fishing rights off the banks of Newfoundland. Here, in the treaty signed at Fontainebleau the third of November 1762, was the foundation stone for an English-speaking America, with England as virtual ruler of the American continent.

The future history of our country was imbedded in that treaty—in that outcome. Several years before, in August 1755, a sermon had been preached before Captain Overton's Independent Company of Volunteers, raised in Hanover County, Virginia. The Evangelist minister who delivered it, Samuel Davies, had been born in New Castle County, Delaware, and would become the fourth president of the College of New Jersey (now Princeton). At the time of his eloquent sermon on *Religion and Patriotism The Constituents of a Good Soldier,* he also became a prophet. "Our Continent is like to become the Seat of War," he intoned, and he added to prophecy a hope. Before he concluded his sermon Davies pointed out "that heroic Youth Col. *Washington,* whom I cannot but hope Providence has hitherto preserved in so signal a manner, for some important service to his Country."

Washington's service to his country, and the course of the American Revolution were revealed only indirectly in the books on our shelves. We left the handling of obvious Americana to the bookseller specialists in the field, and continued nosing out the less obvious. One of the most interesting to us was a pamphlet by the Comte de Mirabeau, his *Avis Aux Hessois Et Autres Peuples de L'Allemagne Vendus par leurs Princes à l'Angleterre—Advice to the Hessians and other people of Germany sold by their princes to England* (1777). This rare ephemeron regards the use of mercenary troops as a form of slavery and dilates on the Hessian troops in the American War of Independence. According to the author, the Prince of Hesse led his subjects into British vessels to be slaughtered in America. Interestingly enough, we purchased that hidden Americanum at an auction in Frankfurt, Germany, and sold it to the Society of the Cincinnati.

We could make discoveries as we traced the course of the American Revolution, not in obvious American histories, but elsewhere, such as in the columns of French newspapers. A run of the *Gazette de France* for the appropriate period becomes an exciting and invaluable source for events across the Atlantic. At one time we had a ten-year run of the *Gazette* from January 1774 to December 1783. And there in its double columns we could read the protests of Boston merchants, accounts of colonial resistance to Parliament, reports of shipping and commerce, affairs monetary and military, the role of the blacks, Franklin's diplomacy in Paris, the American ferment over the importation of tea, the declaration of American independence by the Continental Congress, and even scattered references to that heroic personage named Washington who had been "preserved… for some important service to his Country." From the initial American protests to Cornwallis' surrender at Yorktown, we found the semi-weekly issues of the *Gazette* an unexpectedly rich mine of hidden, now exposed, Americana.

It was not the American colonies but the United States that we found in another run of another French gazette—the *Gazette Générale,* published during the French Revolution. Its motto, "By Nations, Sects, and Parties unconfin'd, / We trace the general annals of mankind," allowed the editors ample space for information from the States, and since we had an almost complete run of this 1790 triweekly, we could catch glimpses of French Revolutionary attitudes toward post-revolutionary America.

George Washington himself helped fix those attitudes. In an anonymous pamphlet, *Etrennes A La Nation,* published at the outset of the French Revolution, we found a printed letter in which George Washington congratulated Lafayette on his ready participation in a worthy cause. Washington was careful to explain the difference in nature between the two revolutions, emphasizing the fact that the defection of the thirteen colonies was inspired by a strong republican spirit determined to break the English bonds of servitude.

Despite the differences between the American and the French Revolutions, the French National Assembly recognized the influence and the importance of the former. In August 1792 that governing body conferred honorary French citizenship upon a number of foreigners including Hamilton, Madison, Paine and George Washington, who, through their writings and their courage, had served the cause of liberty. Among the plethora of *Arrets, Décrets, Déclarations and Proclamations* issued in a deluge of print by Constituent Assembly or National Convention, none is more exhilarating than the *Lois... Qui Confére le titre de citoyens François à plusieurs Etrangers.* George Washington had become not only an honorary citizen of France, but an honorary citizen of the world. The German artist Friedrich Anthing, assembling a collection of one hundred silhouette portraits of the illustrious in 1791, included one American in his gallery of the great—the first President of the United States.

The stature of the United States was acknowledged abroad, along with the reputation of George Washington. In 1798 a physician (Dutasta-Laserre) who had served in the French Revolution wrote a treatise, *Le Code du Bonheur Social* in which he pondered political mysteries. In it he contemplated the superior position of the United States of America which he attributed to the country's geographical isolation, a factor that, according to the author, absolved the country from fear of invasion and from foreign alliance.

By the end of the eighteenth century the United States was clearly trying to establish its independence from Europe. Early in the century, in 1714, the Irish bishop Saint George Ashe, a friend of Jonathan Swift, had delivered a sermon at St. Mary-le-Bow before the Incorporated Society for the Propagation of the Gospel in Foreign Parts. When the sermon was published it was followed by an Abstract of the Society's proceedings which revealed that books had been sent from abroad to New York and elsewhere in an *Attempt towards laying the Foundation of an American Library.* By the end of the century it was clear that a growing national American consciousness was attended by a growing national independence. In 1795, when *A New Introduction to the Latin Language* was prepared by the American clergyman and educator Caleb Alexander, this first collection of its kind in the United States was published so that books needed in American schools did not have to be supplied from abroad. If attempts were to be made toward "laying the foundation of an American library," they would be made on the spot.

Our infrequent forays into the nineteenth century yielded us two appealing examples of hidden Americana. One of them appeared in 1845: an ephemeron still in its original printed wrappers called *An Account of the First Transatlantic Voyage of the Steam Ship Great Britain, Lieut. Hosken, Commander.* In 1845 the *Great Britain,* a screw steamer of enormous size, was considered one of the wonders of the world. But it was not the pamphlet's descriptions of engines and fittings that attracted our interest. Rather, it was the front wrapper of the pamphlet. There, to our delight, we found an advertisement of *furs* supplied by the Hudson's Bay Fur Company and its "emissaries" in "the savage wilds of the vast North American Wildernesses"—priced sable and squirrel boas offered for sale by one John Briscoe. The United States of America was becoming not only increasingly independent but increasingly rich.

As the mid-nineteenth century passed, the United States was also becoming increasingly involved in the horror that would split the republican sons of liberty and divide the country. This too we found in an ephemeral hidden Americanum. George Augustus Henry Sala was an English journalist and artist who drew lithographic plates of the Great Industrial Exhibition of 1850 in London. The architect of the Exhibition, Sir Joseph Paxton, had ordered a memento of it from Sala, and Sala supplied a panorama in comic strip style which he entitled *The House That Paxton Built.* An amusing advertisement, the panorama included sketches of taverns and food supplied by Soyer, the peers and dandies who visited the Exhibition, and the contributions of different countries. Here, alas, was our hidden Americanum. America's "contribution" to the Great Industrial Exhibition was depicted as the planter's armchair of "ebony" supported on slavery.

Europe—especially France—had supplied us with numerous examples of the hidden America we always looked for and sometimes found. The French loved to shape American characters and foibles and events into stage plays or bedtime reading. Sébastien Chamfort had set a one-act verse comedy, *La Jeune Indienne,* in Charleston, an "English colony of America," and regaled his viewers with fascinating references to cannibals, Quakers, and Indians. The great Voltaire had written a novel, *L'Ingénu, Histoire Véritable,* centered about the noble savages of the New World. His *Ingénu* is a Huron Indian whose nobility, though debatable, is intriguing. Utopian romances had long been peppered with bits and pieces of Americana. A *Rélation D'Un Voyage du Pôle Arctique, au Pôle Antarctique, par Le Centre Du Monde* naturally availed itself of American detail in the form of flora and fauna, minerals, caverns, cascades and hot water lakes. One optimistic but anonymous writer described an imaginary voyage to the *Isle D'Eutopie*. That Island of Utopia was located in America.

America, Utopian or bedeviled by slavery, America in its fears and its hopes, in its many colorful and varied aspects, is here, hidden in these books and pamphlets. Their titles do not alert us to the riches buried within. We must scan the pages to find the scattered allusions. Only then, serendipitously, the nuggets are mined, the phrases about discoverer and discovery, about Indian and fur trader, tobacco and herring, a heroic youth named Washington, a planter's armchair of "ebony." We alight upon such words, and the nuggets turn to gold. We too have discovered America.

V
Censorship and Suppression

here is not much hidden, and hence little need for discovery in the areas of censorship, suppression, and persecution. In most of the printed records reading between the lines is not necessary. It is all there—the fears that led to hatred, the prejudices that led to prohibition—in the condemnations and indexes, the arrets and edicts that have crossed our desks. And of all the many-faceted concerns of human minds over the centuries, probably none has called forth more violent censorship than religious faith. A deviation in the worship of God has often led directly not only to the pillory and the block, but to inquisition and expurgation, not only to personal torture, but to literary annihilation. Censorship has been the corollary of almost every departure from established thought. There is scarcely an innovation that has not been followed by a prohibition or an attempt at prohibition. The printed tokens of such sequels have passed through our hands but not from our minds.

On November 7, 1519, the Universities of Cologne and Louvain condemned the heretical doctrine and writings of Martin Luther. Their *Condemnatio,* published around 1520 without indication of place or date, was followed in June 1520 by the Papal Bull *Exsurge* of Leo X, prohibiting what had been condemned. Luther was immediately excommunicated, and at Cologne and Louvain his writings were publicly burned. Our records of that burning began for us the long history of the bigotry of censorship.

Luther's publishers were of course included in the ban on Luther. The Papal Index cites them for punishment, and one Papal Index after another unfolds in an all but unending panorama depicting the shame of shaming. We had the second Index of the Church of Rome, issued in 1559. It banned a stunning array of authors whose writings have been warmly sanctioned by centuries succeeding: Desiderius Erasmus, called the "Stupor Mundi" or "Wonder of the World," author of *The Praise of Folly* whose heroine was identified as a goddess; Abelard, the Catholic monk in love with Eloise; Michael Servetus, who was put to death for his variant opinions. Deviant beliefs and the writings that expounded them were simply not to be printed or circulated, sold or read.

In 1570 Philip II of Spain promulgated an edict forbidding heretical texts; our copy was bound with another Index of prohibited books that expanded the list of the condemned—Luther was joined with Calvin and Zwingli, not to mention Henry VIII who had married too frequently, and Dante who had wandered through Hell. To make sure that the Index of heresy would be internationally understood, it was printed not only in Latin but in French, Dutch and Spanish. To be anti-Catholic was to be banned.

The expurging Index of 1570 was one of the influences that led John Milton to write the *Areopagitica;* so too was the Index of 1599 that included the Talmud among its citations of heretical literature; and so too was the 1631 Papal Index recalling from circulation all suspect works, even writings on judicial astrology. In this *Revocatio* of Pope Urban VIII, published in folio by the Camera Apostolica of Rome, its title-page adorned not only with the papal arms but with woodcuts of St. Peter and St. Paul, it was made very clear that deviant books must be flushed out, brought before the bishop's seat, and used as aids to leaders of the Inquisition. The war on the "ungodly" in print raged on.

In England, a few years before the publication of Milton's *Areopagitica, The First and Large Petition of The City of London* saw print, and there, along with the "publishing and venting of Popish, Arminian and other dangerous Bookes," "lascivious, idle and unprofitable Books and Pamphlets" were condemned—ballads in disgrace of religion, Ovid's "fits of Love," the anonymous and satiric "Parliament of Women." In England, of course, it was the Catholics who suffered censorship and persecution at the hands of the Anglicans. On June 20, 1682, Nathaniel Thompson was sentenced to stand upon the pillory, pay a fine of £100, and subject himself to public abuse. His crime had been the publication and circulation of papist books. Perjured evidence had found him guilty, and the transcript of his trial "for Writing, Printing and Publishing Libels" was sold by us in 1961 to the University of Sydney in Australia.

Overseas in the 1640s, it was the Antinomians who were set up for persecution in a controversy that rocked New England, muzzled the enthusiast Anne Hutchinson, and led to her banishment and eventual death in an Indian massacre. The Antinomian persecution was reported in *A Short Story of the Rise, reign, and ruine of the Antinomians ... that infested the Churches of New-England,* a violent treatise by John Winthrop, first Governor of the Massachusetts Bay Colony, edited by

Thomas Welde, a Puritan divine. Both Church and State joined hands for this particular censorship.

Seventeenth-century France was as active in the pursuit of suppression as England or its colony. The same year as the trial of Nathaniel Thompson—1682—a French verse satire on Jesuit censorship appeared over the graphic title of *Onguant Pour La Brulure ou Le Secret Pour empescher les Jésuites de bruler les livres (Unguent for the Burning or The Secret for Stopping Jesuits from Burning Books)*. But there was not and never had been an unguent for book-burning.

In France in 1598, the Edict of Nantes, signed by King Henry IV, had granted freedom of worship to the Huguenots, members of the reformed faith. By 1685, France changed its mind about these deviants from Catholicism, and the Edict of Nantes was revoked by Henry's descendant, Louis XIV. Louis signed the Revocation in October, denying to Huguenots not only freedom of worship but the pursuit of their crafts and professions. Among the sequence of hampering edicts issued by the French government, we found an *Arrest* that singled out for censorship all Huguenot booksellers and printers. The Huguenot booktrade was to be obliterated. Our copy of the *Arrest* that obliterated it went to the Folger Library.

Perhaps no more stirring example of persecution exists in French history than the eighteenth-century tragedy known as the Calas Affair. It is an affair in which persecution led to literary as well as legal struggle and eventually to a degree of triumph against oppression. It is an example we have cited and discussed before, but its significance is so great that we feel it must become a twice-told tale.*

The story of Jean Calas, a Protestant merchant of Toulouse who became the murdered victim of Catholic fanaticism, is swiftly told. In October 1761, Calas' son Marc-Antoine was found hanged in his father's warehouse. His suicide was interpreted as murder by Toulouse Catholics who claimed that the young man had wished to convert to Rome and had been hanged by his Protestant family. The family, charged with murder, was condemned to the rack. Their appeal to the Toulouse parlement had some success. The family was freed of the charge, but not the father of the family. Jean Calas was now singled out as the Protestant murderer of a son denied espousal of the Catholic faith.

---

*See Leona Rostenberg and Madeleine Stern, *Between Boards: New Thoughts on Old Books* (Santa Monica: Modoc Press, 1989) pp. 107-8.

A DECREE
OF
Starre-Chamber,
CONCERNING
PRINTING,

Made the eleuenth day of July last past. 1 6 3 7.

DIEV ET MON DROIT.

❧ Imprinted at London by *Robert Barker*,
Printer to the Kings most Excellent
Maiestie: And by the Assignes
of *Iohn Bill.* 1 6 3 7.

THE

T R I A L

O F

JOHN PETER ZENGER,

Of New-York, Printer:

Who was charged with having printed and publifhed
a Libel againft the Government; and acquitted.

WITH

A NARRATIVE OF HIS CASE.

To which is now added, being never printed before,

THE TRIAL

O F

Mr. WILLIAM OWEN,

Bookseller, near Temple-Bar,

Who was alfo Charged with the Publication of a Libel
againft the Government; of which he was honour-
ably acquitted by a Jury of Free-born Englifhmen,
Citizens of London.

LONDON:
Printed for J. Almon, oppofite Burlington-Houfe, Piccadilly.
MDCCLXV.
[Price One Shilling.]

Cornerstone of an American Free Press

The trumped-up charge led to a perjured trial; the trial led to an infamous verdict. Calas' last words to his judges protesting his innocence were recorded in a pamphlet entitled *Calas Sur L'Echafaud, A Ses Juges.* In 1762 the verdict was carried out. Jean Calas was broken alive on the wheel and burned to death.

Persecution had been, as it so often is, followed by torture and death. Now the Calas Affair took a different turn. The victim's widow, Dame Anne-Rose Cabibel, took refuge in Switzerland where she enlisted the interest of Voltaire in her husband's murder. During the next three years the aging sceptic of Ferney intervened in the case and converted it into a cause. This transformation was accomplished first with his pen. Voltaire's *Traité sur la Tolerance* was published in Geneva in 1763. The reaction to a judicial murder, it expounded the historical and philosophical aspects of the Calas Affair, the nature of persecution and of religious toleration. Voltaire's *Treatise on Religious Toleration* cried out so loudly against the abuses of intolerance that it led to action. The case was reopened and retried, and in 1765 the Calas family was exonerated, the innocence of Jean Calas established. Eventually the legal position of all French Protestants was improved.

Now the pamphlets proliferated—the memoirs about the participants in the case, the final judgment, the *Ombre De Calas Le Suicide* citing Voltaire as first in the victim's defense. The victim, alas, was still, like his son, an *ombre* (a shade). An English edition of Voltaire's *History of the Misfortunes of John Calas, a Victim to Fanaticism,* published in the epochal year of 1776, included a list of the nobility and gentry who subscribed for the relief of the Calas family. More than a single family had been affected by the Calas Affair. Religious persecution, injustice, the censorship of thought had been exposed. Through the medium of a book a step toward justice had been taken.

If religion takes the lead in prompting censorship, a close second is the political establishment. At least so we gather from the testimony of our bookshelves. Because of our personal interests, our stock reflects the political theory of France, England, and America, countries quick to censure the political philosophy they disapproved of. Almost everything that the Spanish historian Juan de Mariana wrote seems to have incurred blacklisting. France was particularly opposed to his celebrated treatise, *De Rege et Regis Institutione* in which he advocated tyrannicide when necessary. Neither the French Parlement nor the great University of the Sorbonne could tolerate such a belief, and so they joined in stamping it out. On June 8, 1610, Mariana's book espousing its message of violence against tyranny was publicly burned. On the same day an *Arrest* was issued by the Court of Parlement, together with the censure of the Sorbonne. The *Arrest,* an ephemeral pamphlet, records the burning, but at the same time records the importance of what was burned.

In England perhaps one of the most infamous landmarks in the history of censorship is another pamphlet, *A Decree Of Starre-Chamber, Concerning Printing, Made the eleuenth day of July last past. 1637.* The decree is in effect an attempt to abolish a free press by means of oppressive regulations on the Stationers Company. Printers must now affix their names to every item printed; the number of master printers was to be limited to twenty; even the number of apprentices was regulated; one copy of every publication was to be sent to Stationers Hall. The overseers were at work to halt any deviations in political philosophy. The censors were invading Stationers Hall.

Another effective order for "Books Condemned to be Burnt" in England is embodied in a *Judgment & Decree* issued toward the end of the seventeenth century. After the Rye House Plot to murder Charles II and the Duke of York, Oxford University produced the *Judicium & Decretum* of 1683 against pernicious books. Pernicious books were all those books that attacked the divine right theory of kingship, from John Milton's *Eikonoklastes* to Thomas Hobbes' *Leviathan.* The books that opposed the status quo were the "Books Condemned to be Burnt."

Across the seas, during the next century, there was a more promising outcome of a trial for anti-government libel. *The Trial of John Peter Zenger, Of New-York, Printer: Who was charged with having printed and published a Libel against the Government* made history. In this particular case the accused, though charged and tried by his countrymen, was also acquitted by them. The trial has been called "the germ of American freedom, the morning star of that liberty which subsequently revolutionized America." After his apprenticeship to William Bradford, John Peter Zenger founded the *New-York Weekly Journal,* a vehicle for criticism of the government. Both the Governor of New York (Cosby) and his policies were challenged, and consequently printer-journalist Zenger was tried for libel in 1735. His defense by Andrew Hamilton was regarded as the most notable event of the day; his acquittal became the cornerstone of an American free press.

Another trial, held toward the end of the eighteenth century, encompasses for us all three countries: France, England and America. The trial on the part of the king against the author of a libel attacking the royal family took place in December 1792. The king was George III of England. The book charged as libelous—"False, Wicked, Scandalous, and Seditious"—was the *Rights of Man* which had already been adopted as the manifesto of sympathizers with the French Revolution. The author of the book was an American, Thomas Paine. The trial took place at London's Guildhall and was recorded in shorthand. The verdict was "Guilty." Our copy of *The Genuine Trial of Thomas Paine, for A Libel contained in the second part of Rights of Man* bore a frontispiece portrait of Paine and a full-page plate showing the author with his *Rights of Man* surrounded by monkeys.

The history of censorship is also the history of deviation and innovation. The newness in science, in philosophy, in education, is always suspect. The old guard must protect itself against the new. The sequence of the condemned is a sequence of the pioneering great: Grotius on the Index in 1627; Descartes in 1663; Bacon in 1669. Grotius' concept of war and peace; Descartes' views on the supremacy of the intellect; Bacon's advocacy of the new science in his *Advancement of Learning*—all were departures from orthodoxy, candidates for obliteration. Every century provided such candidates. The *Decrees* of the seventeenth century, the *Determinatios, Censures* and *Arrests* of the eighteenth century marked out giants for destruction. The *De L'Esprit* of Helvétius, a milestone in utilitarian philosophy, stressing the natural quality of intelligence and the omnipotence of education, was publicly burned as dangerous doctrine. Rousseau's *Emile,* expounding a new system of education, stressing the inner, natural development of the child, led swiftly to condemnation. According to the *Censure* by the faculty of Theology of Paris, this innovative work was to be torn and burned (lacéré et brulé) at the foot of the great staircase. The author went in exile to Geneva.

Prohibitions were not confined to religious sectarianism or political philosophy or new ideas. Even social customs called forth the fury of the censor, a fury that can be traced in the printed records that have reached our shelves.

A favorite Medici pastime seems to have been the issuance of *Bando* after *Bando* forbidding the playing of cards or marbles, checkers, quoits, any form of gambling in public streets and squares, inns and even private domiciles. Obscenity on the stage was attacked in a vehement work by one Girolamo Fiorentini entitled *Comoedio-Crisis* deploring the insidious demons and "devil's pomp" of the theater and demanding theatrical censorship. In a *Décision* of 1693, the Sorbonne censored comedies and spectacles.

Indeed, the practice of excommunication of dramatists, actors, singers and dancers was longstanding in France. The celebrated actress, Mademoiselle Clairon, of the Comédie Italienne, attempted to have the practice annulled and was extolled for her efforts by the great Voltaire.

In England, decades earlier, stage censorship had received a curious reversal when the stage censor himself was censored. William Prynne, author of *Histrio-Mastix. The Players Scourge,* a denunciation of the drama, incurred the animosity of England's queen who happened to be a stage-loving Frenchwoman, sister to Louis XIII. She herself had participated in a dramatic performance, and consequently Star Chamber ruled that Prynne be fined, imprisoned and branded, not to mention relieved of his ears.

In the United States, even after the Zenger trial, censorship persisted through the centuries. There Anthony Comstock assumed the self-appointed role of censor of the nineteenth century. Comstock of course censored anything that smacked to him of immorality, from newspapers to story papers, from dime novels to half-dime novels. His *Traps for the Young* of 1883 entraps for us the "dangers" that aroused his ferocious and tireless opposition.

Like social customs and so-called immoralities, political and historical events called forth literature that suffered censorship. When the English throne was claimed by the unfortunate Mary of Scots, a French writer, Belleforest, leaped to her defense in 1572, supporting her cause. His book, *L'Innocence De... Madame Marie Royne d'Escosse,* was naturally forbidden circulation in England. Worse still, when the title was discovered in the shop of an English stationer William Carter, the bookseller was seized, tried, found guilty of treason, and hanged.

Prior to modern times few historical events have excited more printed bans than the French Revolution and the concepts and episodes that foreshadowed it.

Early on—in 1736—the counselor of state, René Hérault, pronounced a *Judgment* condemning a group (one woman included) for establishing a clandestine printing press and printing subversive works. His *Jugement* named names along with the places where their printing tools and fonts had been found. Three specific works were ordered burned, among them one very aptly named *La vérité persécutée (Truth persecuted)*.

Prior to the Revolution, between 1770 and 1789, the French government seems to have sensed the troubles that lay ahead. We once had in our possession a single volume bound in boards that contained 23 *Arrets* of the Parlement or the King's Counsel of State suppressing the writings of practically all the great philosophes whose doctrine shaped the background of the French Revolution. Raynal was one of them, condemned for his multivolume history of commerce in the two Indies—now described as blasphemous and heretical. Mirabeau was another, his *Lettre* on banking, his work on Necker, his history of the Court of Berlin, interpreted as anti-government. Linguet's periodical *Annales Politiques* was suppressed as anti-royalist. A *Lettre* by Volney was destined for laceration and burning. The entire edition of the *Almanach des honnêtes gens* was to be burned in 1788, and its author, a distinguished litterateur Sylvain Maréchal, was to be imprisoned. All because on one leaf he had substituted the names of eminent personages for saints' names. The government of Louis XVI smelled trouble and was running scared. The cudgel it used was censorship.

By the 1790s the Revolutionary Tribunal was using a similar cudgel, using it not only against books but against their authors, and against farmers and merchants, bakers and lawyers, aristocrats and rebels. The burning of books was now accompanied by the removal of heads. During the Terror the guillotine became the companion of the bonfire. The lists of those condemned by judgment or decree, their names coupled with their ages, their professions, their districts and their "crimes," provide bloody sources, poignant records of the nature not only of the French Revolution but of the persecution and censorship that preceded and followed it.

When, in 1794, a motion was brought before the National Convention of France on the subject of an unrestricted free press, Méhée de La Touche, a writer who had fled to England during the Revolution, wrote a pamphlet expounding his point of view. In *La Queue De Robespierre (The Tail of Robespierre)* he expressed his opposition to the idea. An unrestricted free press, he considered, would not only bring before the public the writings of such dissidents as Voltaire, Rousseau and Helvétius, but seduce mankind. There are beliefs, he held, that should not be printed. Such was the chaotic nature of the time that most copies of *La Queue De Robespierre* were seized in an action that applied censorship to an advocate of censorship.

There were—and for centuries there had been—those who disagreed with Méhée de La Touche—a long line of champions of an unrestricted free press whose legacy is the "liberty to argue freely according to conscience," to know that "truth crushed to earth will rise again." Probably the greatest of these defenders of a free press was John Milton. We never owned the first edition of the *Areopagitica*. We did have Edward Arber's excellent 1849 edition, as well as the lovely edition bound in vellum and issued by Cobden-Sanderson's Doves Press in 1907. The immediate occasion for the writing of *Areopagitica* was of course that 1637 *Decree Of Starre-Chamber* that was once on our shelves, as well as the 1643 "Order of the Lords and Commons Assembled in Parliament" requiring that all books be licensed by an official censor before publication.

As a result of those two restraints, the *Areopagitica* appeared in 1644, the greatest of all pleas for freedom of the press that likens a good book with "reason itself" and the "precious life-blood of a master-spirit." Milton's unforgettable words resounded in the mind of Mirabeau when in 1788 he wrote his *Sur La Liberté De La Presse, Imité De L'Anglois, De Milton*. Basing his thoughts upon the *Areopagitica,* Mirabeau applied Milton's concepts to the exigencies of his own troubled time, discussing government surveillance of books, the history of censorship, and the necessity of a free press as a guaranteed right.

Throughout the French Revolution and in the decades after it, infringements upon the liberty of printing were countered by pleas for liberty. Some were anonymous; others were authored by the French publicist Lanthenas; the distinguished critic La Harpe; Lafayette; Chateaubriand. Their writings championed the rights of author, bookseller and printer, along with the right of anonymity. As Lafayette put it,

AREOPAGITICA;
A SPEECH OF MR. JOHN MILTON FOR THE LIBERTY OF UNLICENC'D PRINTING, TO THE PARLAMENT OF ENGLAND.

ΤΟΥΛΕΥΘΕΡΟΝ Δ' 'ΕΚΕΙΝΟ, 'ΕΙ ΤΙC ΘΕΛΕΙ ΠΟΛΕΙ
ΧΡΗCΤΟΝ ΤΙ ΒΟΥΛΕΥΜ' 'ΕΙC ΜΕCΟΝ ΦΕΡΕΙΝ, 'ΕΧΩΝ.
ΚΑΙ ΤΑΥΘ' 'Ο ΧΡΗΙΖΩΝ, ΛΑΜΠΡΟC 'ΕCΘ', 'Ο ΜΗ ΘΕΛΩΝ
CΙΓΑΙ, ΤΙ ΤΟΥΤΩΝ 'ΕCΤΙΝ 'ΙCΑΙΤΕΡΟΝ ΠΟΛΕΙ;

Euripid. Hicetid.

This is true Liberty when free born men
Having to advise the public may speak free,
Which he who can, and will, deserv's high praise,
Who neither can nor will, may hold his peace;
What can be juster in a State than this?

"Truth Crushed to Earth Will Rise Again"

a free press would sustain the liberty of the people and advance the propagation of new ideas.

Everywhere censorship and pleas for liberty continued their antiphonal course. In Paris in 1827, 230 printers and booksellers (Honoré de Balzac among them) petitioned against censorship of the press. In Alton, Illinois, a decade later, the press of the abolitionist printer Elijah Lovejoy was destroyed and he himself was killed. Lovejoy was "murdered in defence of the liberty of the press." But somehow that liberty, like Milton's "good book" could not be killed.

Through the centuries, as the struggle between suppression and emancipation continued, scholars have drawn censorship into their areas of study. As early as 1736 a doctoral dissertation by a German legal student discussed banned books. In 1768 a bibliographical treatise on censored writings was published in Leipzig. In England *A Catalogue Of Curious but Prohibited Books ... Chiefly Modern* appeared in the mid-eighteenth century that made fun of the subject, listing several imaginary titles: "Villany the Best Policy," "Germany the true Sinking-Fund," "The Art of Not Thinking," "The Works of a Celebrated Foreign Lady, Stitch'd, or in Sheets," and "Modern Nobility. (Newest Edition, very cheap)."

There is little that has not triggered some form of censorship. If the contents of books have not occasioned banning, a trivial cause, such as use of a false imprint, has. According to a 1671 Paris decree, the great Dutch publisher Daniel Elzevier contravened a mandate forbidding imaginary imprints when he issued *L'Aimable Mère de Jésus* by the Jesuit Professor in Madrid, Father Juan Eusebio Nieremberg. Actually printed in Leyden by Elzevier, the work bore a fictitious Amiens imprint. Consequently, the entire shipment of copies was seized and confiscated by the Paris authorities. As a result, *L'Aimable Mère de Jésus* is one of the scarcest publications of the seventeenth century. Our copy went to Harvard in 1952.

It is the ultimate irony in the history of censorship that works on censorship have themselves been subjected to censure. In 1775 the French publicist Linguet wrote his *Théorie du Libelle,* discussing the effects of libel, especially of libelous books and brochures. In an *Arrest* of the King's Counsel of State, the government, regarding the work as calumny, pro-

hibited all booksellers, printers and colporteurs from selling or distribut-
ing it. If a study of libel could be censured, anything could be censured.

The struggle between censorship and freedom would continue
even into the twentieth century when the bonfires of Nazi Germany
burned books as its gaschambers extinguished bodies. We must forever
remind ourselves of those "winds of doctrine" that John Milton wrote
about, and reassure ourselves that, in the grappling of Truth and
Falsehood, "who ever knew Truth put to the worse in a free and open
encounter?"

VI

Stratagems of Satan

*I*t was a writer forced to flee his country and intimate with the demons of persecution who coined the evocative phrase, the *Stratagems of Satan*. Those stratagems were multifarious and far-reaching both in time and in space, and they occasioned a body of literature that is often fantastic and unbelievable. We acquired some of it in editions that sprang from three centuries.

Born in the year of discovery, 1492, the Italian Jacopo Aconzio abandoned Catholicism for Protestantism and sought refuge in Protestant England. When in 1565 he wrote a book entitled *Stratagematvm Satanae,* he consequently dedicated it to Queen Elizabeth. Since Aconzio's purpose was to further tolerance among divergent religious sects, he devoted more space to apostasy and heresy than to orthodoxy, and in this connection revealed what he had learned about the stratagems of Satan. Demonology and divination attracted his learned attention, and he concerned himself especially with the influence of Satan upon man. The stratagems of Satan would color much of the thinking from the Renaissance even into the Age of Enlightenment.

Actually Satan had exercised his stratagems long before the Renaissance. Had not the medieval Robert Duke of Normandy been born in answer to prayers to the devil and been named Robert the Devil for his "monstrous birth and behavior"? Satan's powers were unquestioned by many even before the invention of printing by movable type. It was the sixteenth century, however, that was especially alive to the Stratagems of Satan, which swiftly developed into a branch of learning that might be called the science of unscience.

Scanning the Renaissance treatises that have come our way, we can round up the diabolical intents and purposes of Satan as we cogitate the strange beliefs of our authors. We find at least one, a lawyer from Piacenza, who held that the devil was bound in Hell and could not vex mankind until the advent of the anti-Christ. Most of the others thought the devil was quite free to vex mankind. The devil was empowered to possess the human soul and strangle the pious, to intermingle with "corrupted senses and phantasy." From the "boutique de Satan" could spread disease and even the assassin's art; witches, who had insensible spots on their bodies, were of course in league with the devil; the stratagems of Satan could pervade home and court, animal and human, male and female, body and mind.

And so the writers, Italian and French, reformers and teachers, savants and jurists, physicians, theologians and philosophers, developed during the sixteenth century the pseudoscience of demonology and magic, witchcraft and sorcery, divination and prognostication, and perhaps even psychiatry. They repeated one another in their treatises and dialogues, but they added innovative stitches to the fabric too. One by one the necromancers wove their spells as we turned the pages of their books.

A treatise by Paolo Grillando appeared early in the century but was reprinted at the century's end, testifying to a persistent interest in his subject—prophecies. The author elaborated on the close relations between demons and witches; witches, he held, could not shed tears—a fortunate disability in light of what later happened to many of them. He rounded out his study with an endorsement of chiromancy as a natural science. Around 1540, one Otho Lupano added to the literature with his *Torricella Dialogo,* a dialogue on most of the aspects of Satanism, from the forms and appearances of spirits and demons to magic and its portents.

At the mid-century, the French pamphleteer Pierre Viret took on the whole supernatural world for his province, tracking down the essence of the devil and exploring the nature of superstition, truth and falsehood into the bargain. His satanic net was wide, finding room for Epicurean philosophy, papist doctrine, and the vanity of idols. In addition, he introduced to his readers the various kinds of white and black demons as well as a cabal of devils and their evil influence. Another mid-century writer, Merula, found room in his *Memorabilivm ... opus* for discussions of celestial and demonic powers, critical days, the seven stages of man, and the transmigration of souls, as well as poisons and sex mutations. The devil was truly tireless. A collected volume of five Italian investigations "super Maleficiis" published in 1560 indicated that murder was the outcome of demonic activity. The authors' cogitations seem to resonate from the meeting of some sixteenth-century psychiatric association!

Lambert Daneau, a Calvinist who taught theology at Geneva, wrote a dialogue in 1574: *Les Sorciers,* in which he offered a moderate view on the subject of sorcerers and their powers, their aid in times of sickness, condemnations of them and precautions against them. He discusses, too, the cases of sorcery under consideration by the Parlement of Paris, cases that would multiply and extend significantly into the next century. The nature and conduct of witches engaged the erudite attention of the Swiss scholar Thomas Erastus, who dilated on their relations with demons. Demons, he informed his readers, could somehow assume the shape of bodies without actual flesh. Witches, he concluded, should be executed.

Demons and witches and the attitude of the church toward them continued to preoccupy many sixteenth-century Italian and French scholars. Probably the most influential text of the time was the *IIII. Ljvres Des Spectres Ov Apparitions Et Visions D'Esprits* produced in 1586 by Pierre Le Loyer of Angers. Le Loyer took pains to analyze the role and identification of witches, demons and spectres. Of particular interest is his allusion to the disordered imagination in the individual and its consequences. Surely his work is itself a spectre and forecast of twentieth-century psychiatric concerns.

The devil's power was obviously so great that a pact with the devil seemed a wise and productive undertaking. Of all such pacts perhaps none is better known than the one formed by the sixteenth-century magician Faust. The *History of the Damnable and Deserved Death of Dr. John Faustus* was an enormously popular work that went through several editions. We owned the French translation by Palma Cayet, where we read of Faust's life and death, his pact with the devil, his diabolical blasphemies and bacchanalia. The account of his life would influence a host of later writers on diabolical themes in general and the Faust legend in particular, from Goethe to Louisa May Alcott, whose *Modern Mephistopheles* carried the theme of pact with the devil well into the nineteenth century.

Toward the end of the sixteenth century, a Spanish savant, Pereira, joined the bevy of French and Italians by producing an encyclopedic occult treatise that covered magic and divination by astrology, predictions and the casting of nativities. Necromancy and alchemy, oracles and prodigies punctuated his work which did not fail to include a study of dream interpretation that suggested strong modern overtones. Around the same time, a distinguished German physician-philosopher, Caspar Peucer, examined with Germanic thoroughness the various kinds of divination—lot-casting, medical prognostications, prodigies and portents, divination from the entrails of animals, and dream interpretation.

Before the century was over, proof was offered that disease and death could both result from satanic influence. An Italian physician, Codronchi, who practiced medicine in Imola and wrote the first treatises on diseases of the larynx and forensic medicine, also wrote a book in 1595, *De Morbis Veneficiis,* on the diseases supposedly caused by witchcraft. The most interesting were those related to fertility and infertility: impotence, sterility, and abortion. For such ailments Codronchi recommended natural remedies, from baths and emetics to oils, liniments and suffumigations. In the same year of 1595, a brochure was issued relating an attack upon the life of Henry IV of France that had taken place on December 27, 1594. The Jesuits were held responsible for the failed attempt, but it is made perfectly clear that the would-be assassin had learned his evil and murderous ways from what was styled the "boutique de Satan."

The "boutique de Satan" continued its malevolent activity after the turn of the century. Jean Maldonat's *Traicté des Anges et Démons,* written earlier, was published early in the century, assuring a new generation that, despite Satan's ability to infest and corrupt the human body, angels would win in the power struggle with demons. The influence of spirits on human behavior absorbed Henry de Montagu, a squire from La Costa, who added to Satan's lore with his *Daemonis Mimica* of 1612. There he investigated such matters as oracles by water, wine and blood, pyromancy and "diabolical mimicries." Another Frenchman, a poet-lawyer of Bordeaux, Pierre Trichet, followed through with musings on centaurs and magic rites, divination and books of magic.

By 1634, there was a solid literary and presumably scholarly background for the pseudoscience of demonology. Its practices had been investigated and described, categorized and organized into a vast body of misinformation. 1634 was a crucial year in Satanic history. On August 18, a priest of the Church of Sainte-Croix in Loudun, France, was burned alive for practicing the satanic stratagem of witchcraft.

The priest, Urbain Grandier, born in 1590, was accused of demonic practices by a group of Ursuline novices of the Carmelite Convent. The nuns traced the beginning of Grandier's sacrilegious crimes to 1632 when he had first taken demonic "possession" of them. The great Richelieu joined in the conspiracy, and the case of the "Devils of Loudun" began its tragic course. That course was accompanied by a series of books and pamphlets that reanimate the diabolical history. In the *Interrogatoire* of

1634, details of Grandier's practice of witchcraft were traced up to June 23, 1634 by the commission appointed to investigate the accusations. The report included a list of the judges appointed in the case. The act of condemnation of August 18, 1634 enumerated preceding acts in the Loudun "sorcery," and placed Urbain Grandier directly at the stake. This *Extraict des Registres de la Commission ordonnée par le Roy. Povr Le Ivgement ... de Maistre Vrbain Grandier* we found in 1971 on the shelves of a dealer just outside Munich—an appropriate location for this horrendous sentence. A *Récit Véritable de ce Qvi S'Est Passé A Lovdvn* summed up the crime and its punishment. In addition, Nicolas Aubin, a French Protestant who sought refuge in Holland after the Revocation of the Edict of Nantes, reviewed the Loudun case toward the end of the century. His *Histoire des Diables de Loudun* surveys Grandier's so-called possession of the Ursuline nuns, their accusations of witchcraft against him, Richelieu's conspiracy, and the burning at the stake in 1634. It provides the major source for the affair; it also provided a source for Aldous Huxley's twentieth-century novel, *The Devils of Loudun,* and the Broadway play based on it. It is important to remind ourselves that the original "Devils of Loudun" was neither novel nor play, but stark, satanic history.

Public interest in the subject continued. In 1653, François Perreaud, the French demonographer—study of the stratagems of Satan had become a veritable profession—compiled an extensive survey on demonology in which he touched upon the powers of evil spirits over past, present and future, illusions, and demonic influence on senses and soul. He added to his *Démonologie* another treatise, *L'Antidémon de Mascon,* a case history of a demon's activity in the author's home. Perreaud seemed to be heading straight in the direction of Sigmund Freud and another science or pseudoscience called psychiatry.

The last execution for sorcery by the Paris Parlement occurred at Pacy in 1691. A few years later the *Factums, et Arrest* of the Paris Parlement regarding the case in which shepherds at Pacy had been accused of bewitching animals was published. The great historian of magic, Lynn Thorndike, dismisses the accusation of "bewitching animals at Pacy" as "an utterly absurd and incredible tale." But Mr. Thorndike was apparently completely unaware of our *Factums, et Arrest Du Parlement de Paris, Contre des Bergers Sorciers Executez ... dans la Province de Brie*—an almost contemporary record of the event.

DÆMONOLOGIA;

hoc est,

ADVERSVS INCAN-
tationem siue Magiam,

INSTITVTIO,

FORMA DIALOGI
concepta, & in Libros III.
distincta:

Authore

SERENISSIMO POTEN-
tissimoq, Principe, Dn. IACOBO,
*Dei gratiâ Angliæ, Scotiæ, Hy-
berniæ, ac Franciæ Rege, fidei defensore,* &c.

EX ANGLICO QVIDEM
sermone per *Vincentium Meuseuotium* in
Belgicum; nunc verò è Belgico in La-
tinum conuersa, operâ *M.
Herman. Germbergii.*

HANOVIÆ
Apud Guilielmum Antonium,

MDCIV.

"The Wisest Fool in Christendom" versus Satan

Just as observers reported the witchcraft of the day, they also reported the attempts to eradicate witchcraft. There seem to have been two major methods of eradication. One was exorcism; the other, writings by anti-demonographers.

Actually, exorcism was aimed at eradicating the effects of witchcraft rather than witchcraft itself. Compendiums and manuals were compiled, designed to record the history and nature of the art of exorcism. It was necessary to recognize the presence of malignant spirits, their types and apparitions, their methods of entering the bodies of the possessed. Exorcists must ascertain whether an individual was afflicted with physical disease or possessed by demons. Formulas for the expulsion of spirits, incubi, succubi, their satellites and associates, were provided. Special methods were suggested for specific expulsions, such as ejecting demons from marriage and the home, from winds and serpents, even from milk and butter. The exorcists who passed through our hands operated from the end of the sixteenth century to the mid-seventeenth, and hailed mostly from Italy or France. One—Eynatten, author of a *Manvale Exorcismorvm*—was canon of the Cathedral of Antwerp. All gave themselves tirelessly to the casting out of devils.

Among our anti-demonologists, Giovanni Francesco Pico della Mirandola, the distinguished Italian humanist, takes precedence. Pico's dialogue entitled *La Strega* first appeared in Latin as *Strix* in 1523 and, in addition to discussing dreams and portents, auguries and predictions, he boldly attacked magic and its diabolical arts. A Belgian physician, Johann Wier, later joined the foes of demonology, adding ammunition to the onslaught. Without actually questioning the existence of demons, Wier's *De Praestigiis Daemonum* and his *De Lamiis* attacked their impostures and magic illusions. Opposed to the superstitions of his age, he regarded witches as deranged persons whose imaginations had been corrupted by demons, and who therefore were not guilty of heresy but rather were insane. Johann Wier set other matters straight too. Among his more portentous findings was his conclusion that women supposedly possessed by the devil were actually hysterical or melancholic, a diagnosis that may well have reached the ears of Sigmund Freud.

As the sixteenth century wound to its close, the *Daemonologia* of James I of England appeared, not only denouncing witchcraft but exhorting civil power to suppress it. His great contribution to anti-Satanism was divided into three books, the first on magic or necromancy, the second on sorcery or witchcraft, and the third on spirits and the punishment of witches. We had this important work by the "wisest fool in Christendom" in the Latin translation of 1604. We displayed it at the first antiquarian book fair in this country held in 1960, where it attracted the attention of a private collector who purchased it. As a result, any demons we may have harbored were happily expelled, and our spirits rose to lofty heights.

Interest in the stratagems of Satan did not end with James I's denunciation. Indeed, it survived well into the eighteenth century. An erudite treatise on demons, *Mysterivm de Daemonibvs,* by a German mathematician and philosopher, Frobesius, found a place on our shelves. In it the author traced concepts of demons from Socrates and Plato, analyzed their orders and classes as well as their habitats in the human body, and even attempted a bit of pioneer psychiatric investigation. As late as 1792, another German, the publicist Karl von Eckhartshausen, who delved in magic on the side, wrote a hair-raising study of phantoms and ghosts, poltergeists and demonological visions. The finely engraved frontispiece of his book shows a sleeping damsel whose slumbers will shortly be disturbed by a skeleton, a black cat, and an ape-like vampire.

Damsels, sleeping or awake, do not fare well in most of the literature devoted to Satanism that has passed through our hands. Their most conspicuous role seems to be that of accuser, as in the case of the Devils of Loudun when the Ursuline nuns charged Urbain Grandier with their demonic "possession." The sex's only apologist in our collections was Johann Wier who described women possessed by the devil as simply hysterical or melancholic. Not a single work on demonology that we have bought, studied and sold was written by a woman.

Apparently our women writers seem to have left the field of demonology almost entirely to men and, in place of writing about evil spirits and magic influences, concentrated upon the events and problems of the world they lived in. The pens of feminist authors seem to have been guided less by Satan and his stratagems than by Minerva and her wisdom.

VII

Feminism

*F*eminism and women's rights were not uppermost in the minds of most of our early champions of women. Male Renaissance writers wrote glowingly on the subject of the female sex, but they wrote less about women as human beings, as potential doers and achievers, than about woman as the embodiment of beauty, morality, and obedience. There was little need for such writers to remind their readers of the traditional association of woman with children, home, and church. That went without saying. The woman they delineated had little to do with the stress and turmoil of the world. Confined to the home, she could be safely placed on a pedestal, a symbol of virtuous acquiescence. Yet those writings by male supporters of the sex would eventually extend the audience for writings by women and clear the ground for the concept of women's rights.

Egalitarianism was indeed a long way off, but in a way it began on our shelves—with a tribute to woman by a French writer published in 1505. It was that early that François Le Roy wrote a little book that he called *Le Liure de la femme forte et Vertueuse (Book of the Stalwart and Virtuous Woman).* This was, to be sure, an encomium to woman by a male supporter, but it singled out for praise the Biblical attributes of virtue and so enthroned woman. In effect, Le Roy based his commentary upon Proverbs and the Song of Songs, linking the female sex directly with Biblical concepts of beauty and purity.

The writers who followed him were similarly inclined to elevate woman. Heinrich Bebel, poet-laureate of the Holy Roman Empire, wrote shortly before his death in 1516 a poem, *Trivmphvs Veneris (The Triumph of Venus),* one book of which was devoted to the "Foemineus Sexus." Renaissance glorifiers of women formed a sizable group who, for the most part, attributed to women such qualities as fortitude and prudence, charity and magnanimity, qualities that raised them far above mundane and earthly goings-on. Time and again, as we scanned the pages by our men defenders of women, we found such virtues emphasized. The Italian savants Capella and Bruni joined forces with a host of others whose vision of woman was somewhat less than realistic.

It was a vision based largely upon their knowledge of women of ancient times or mythology from Sappho to Cleopatra, from Dido to

Penelope, from Minerva to Andromache. Sometimes—as in the case of Dardano's *Bella e Dotta Difesa delle Donne* of 1554, the Amazons were included in the frame of reference. Toward the end of the century, the French writers Jean de Marconville and Pont-Aymery followed suit, citing classical authorities and Amazonian allusions in their efforts to prove woman's superiority over man. Pont-Aymery's book on the subject was translated into English in 1599 as "A Woman's Woorth defended against all the Men in the World."

It was Jean de Marconville, writing on the *Bonté et Mavvaistie des Femmes* (the *Good and Bad of Women)* who upheld as a symbol of good Joan of Arc, and as a symbol of evil Pope Joan. It was he too who eulogized not only women warriors such as Joan of Arc, but women disguised as men who became great property owners! For the most part, Renaissance man in praise of woman continued to laud woman's role at home, not in the world. Even the distinguished Spanish humanist Vives who tutored the English Princess Mary, viewed woman's education, reading and intellectual pursuits as part and parcel of her duties to husband and family. Supportive and forward-looking as he was, Vives saw women less as individuals than as daughters, wives and widows. Their training must hence be connected to their relations with children, the instruction of youth, the management of the home. Woman's marital duties, her administration of the household, her conduct during widowhood, her general behavior were subjects about which macho males of the sixteenth and seventeenth centuries waxed eloquent. Woman's status as wife or widow formed sections of most books by men in praise of women, an entire work on the subject: *Dialoghi Del Matrimonio e vita Vedouile* by Bernardo Trotto, appearing in 1578.

In the course of such commentaries much was written on the more trivial aspects of women's lives. An Italian bishop writing in the 1520s— Gorio Gherio—concentrated upon the costume and dowry of the Renaissance lady, even delving into the ornaments, the gold and silver she should favor and the materials of her costume. The immodesty of woman's dress was a delectable subject for Antoine Estienne, whose *Rémonstrance Charitable* on their dissolute ornaments was published anonymously in 1577. His remonstrance, though far from "charitable," was all-embracing, including satins, taffetas and velours, panaches, earrings and bracelets, hair styling and the use of false hair. No bishop but the Pope himself—Sixtus V—issued a 1587 decree on dress reform espe-

cially for wives and widows—*Riforma del Vestire*—in which he listed prohibited articles of clothing and ornaments and prescribed costume for
feasts and banquets, weddings and funerals. Writing a century later
another bishop, the Bishop of Winchester, produced *A Discourse of
Artificial Beauty ... Between Two Ladies* whose dialogue touched upon
such trivia as "painting, patching and powdering." The author defined
cosmetic improvement as a badge of vanity and a mark of pride.

It was the women who eschewed "painting, patching and powdering," exercised the Biblical virtues, and applied whatever they learned to
home management, who were the subjects of most of our early books by
men in praise of women. The seventeenth century followed the line of
the sixteenth with such telling titles as *Della Eccellenza delle Donne,
L'Honnêste Femme,* and *Haec Homo: Wherein The Excellency of the
Creation of Woman is described.* Only a few male champions held a less
abstract, more analytic, penetrating and positive view of the powers and
capabilities of the opposite sex. One was the Cartesian philosopher
Poullain de La Barre who actually accepted sexual equality, exposing the
false arguments of his adversaries in an anonymous work misleadingly
titled *L'Excellence Des Hommes, contre L'Egalité Des Sexes.*

The German author of a *Defensio sexus muliebris,* writing in 1595,
had been more forthright and courageous. Simon Gediccus, a theologian
and true feminist, published his treatise to refute a work by one "Valens
Acidalius" (surely an appropriate pseudonym) in which it was concluded
that women were not human. In his defense of the *sexus muliebris,* Herr
Gediccus disagreed, answering the question, "Are Women Human?" in
the affirmative.

It took women themselves to prove not only their humanity, but
their abilities and powers, their egalitarianism, and their very special creativity. There is no doubt that some women writers patterned their output on the encomia of their male admirers. Even the titles they used seem
derivative: *La Nobilta, Et L'Eccellenza delle Donne* by Lucrezia Marinella
in 1601, the *Apologie des Dames* by Madame Galien de Chateau-Thierry,
who signed herself "M. de ***" in 1748. Like their male models, these
women cited in support of their views the heroines of Scripture and history and ended up with imitative eulogies of their sex.

For the most part, however, the writings by women that crossed
our desks were far more original in nature and enterprising in scope.
These women seem to have experimented with almost every literary

genre. The poets outranked them all, at least quantitatively. One of our earlier versifiers, the Renaissance Italian Gaspara Stampa, who was also a musician, sang her lines to the accompaniment of a lute. Known as the Sappho of her time, she fell in love with Count Collalto of Treviso who abandoned her for another. Thus she had much emotion to express in her sonnets and madrigals which were published posthumously by her sister after the writer's untimely death at age 30. The signora's *Rime* first appeared in 1554, and our stock boasted not only that first edition but a reprint edition of 1738 edited by her eighteenth-century compatriot, the Venetian woman poet Luisa Bergalli. In that later edition, Count Collalto's own verses are included, along with frontispiece portraits of himself and the lover he abandoned.

Gaspara Stampa had been preceded by one of the most illustrious Italian Renaissance poets, Vittoria Colonna whose love life was equally unfortunate. She had been married at age 17 to the worthless Marquis of Pescara and did not write her sonnets on music, religious faith and church reform until after his death. Her poems were prized by Michelangelo who praised them enthusiastically. They are still prized today.

Several of the women poets who graced our shelves were both musicians and writers who wrote their verses in praise of their illustrious friends. Tullia d'Aragona of Naples, for example, indited her sonnets to the distinguished Bembo and Varchi; the bluestocking Isabella Cervoni eulogized Henry IV of France and his wife Marie de Medici; the Roman Signora Margherita Costa, who resided in the court of the Grand Duke Ferdinand II de Medici, expressed her love affair with Tuscany in her idyls and love poems to members of the Medici family. One volume of her writings was entitled *Il Violino*.

Elisabetta Sirani, who was poisoned at the age of 27, was an artist, not a poet, but she was the source of poems by others. After her untimely demise in 1665 a volume of poems by Italian academicians appeared, not to exalt her nobility or her virtue, but to honor her for the works of art she had created in her short but productive life. A distinguished woman painter, she had been a follower of Guido Reni whose masterpieces are sometimes confused with hers, and in whose tomb she was buried.

Philosophy engaged the concentrated attention of several of our early women writers. Our Neapolitan poet Tullia d'Aragona took up her pen to write not only sonnets, but a dialogue on the infinity of love.

Centuries later, in 1777, a most unusual woman known only as Mademoiselle de Chanterolle discussed in her *Aspect philosophique* the attitudes of the French philosophes on Rousseauean society as a source of happiness. She took pains to evaluate seriously the weaknesses and the strengths of women, and her maxims are still quotable: "It is better to be the oppressed than the oppressor"; "ennui follows ignorance"; "a good society consists of people conserving mutual liberty."

The keys to philosophy or natural philosophy were penetrated by another eighteenth-century woman, Sabine Stuart de Chevalier, born in Scotland and. married to a French scholar. Sabine wrote her *Discours Philosophique sur Les Trois Principes, Animal, Végétal et Minéral* in 1781. In it she explored problems in natural philosophy, chemistry, alchemy, the transmutation of metals, the nature of earth and of fire. This remarkable work is adorned with two plates by the author herself, one depicting an allegorical scene, the other the interior of a laboratory.

Letters and memoirs, dramas, novels and criticism are genres of writing which women have enriched through the centuries. From the medieval nun Hroswitha of Gandersheim, author of six comedies, to Mary Wollstonecraft Shelley, who became a hack writer after Shelley's death, the literary shelves of every library in the world are filled with the outpourings of women. The subjects of their books are all-encompassing; many of them reflect accurately the tastes and preoccupations of their times, from a Renaissance court to the French Revolution; still more reflect the thoughts and emotions of their writers, and thus mirror the life of half the human race.

Between Boards, a book we co-authored in 1977, includes a chapter entitled "Feminism is Collectible." In it we discussed and listed 117 books by and about women. Now, some twenty years later, we can write a chapter on feminism markedly unlike that earlier chapter, in which we refer to altogether different books by and about women. In the two decades that have passed since the first publication of *Between Boards,* we have acquired so many additional books by and about women that we can address the same subject without repetition. The varied and prolific nature of feminist writing needs no other testimony.

Writing has always been an acceptable occupation for women. No revolutionary ardor or reform spirit was required for a woman to dip pen into ink and create a poem or shape a romance. Not all women who produced books, however, were professional writers. Some who left written records of their work were practitioners in non-literary fields. And a few of them, early on, dared to enter non-traditional occupations.

Women artists were almost if not quite as acceptable as women writers. Antoinette Bouzonnet Stella hailed from a distinguished family of engravers; yet it took some innovativeness for her to produce in 1675 her *Frise faicte sur les desseins de J. Romaine,* a series of engravings based upon those of Giulio Romano at the village of Te near Mantua. Just so, Elisabeth, daughter of the calligraphic engraver Louis Senault, published an exquisitely engraved prayerbook whose delicate floral and arabesque designs, vignettes and ornamentation testify to her taste and skill. We had a copy of her *Hevres Nouvelles* issued around 1700, bound in red gilt morocco, and including Elisabeth's extraordinary dedication to the Dauphin in which she discussed the difficulties surmounted by one of her youth and sex.

The printing trades attracted many women, several of whom were given temporary residence in our quarters. Widows of printer-publishers who carried on their spouses' enterprises are too numerous to mention. But in eighteenth-century Paris, Mademoiselle Louise-Félicité Kéralio formed—not a marital union—but a business partnership with Jean Lagrange in order to publish books. Mademoiselle Kéralio was not only a publisher but a scholar and an author. The Kéralio and Lagrange imprint appeared on her own *Histoire D'Elisabeth, Reine D'Angleterre,* a five-volume study in which one feminist reanimated the life of another.

In England in the nineteenth century the Victoria Press, whose policy was to employ women printers, was founded by a woman, Emily Faithfull. Faithfull paid *Three Visits to America,* and her book on the subject discussed from personal observation the American work force and non-traditional employment for women. The first woman publisher in Boston, Elizabeth Palmer Peabody, reformer and transcendentalist, had opened in 1840 at 13 West Street a bookstore that became "one of the most unusual and influential ... in American history." Among the earliest of her imprints was a pamphlet on antislavery, *Emancipation,* by the distinguished Unitarian clergyman William E. Channing for whom Peabody had earlier served as copyist. Our copy of *Emancipation* opened up for us the beginnings of women in American publishing.

There were far more women book canvassers than book publishers. Especially after the Civil War and well into the nineteenth century, women bearing prospectuses of forthcoming publications wandered the country to enlist advance purchasers. We had a publishers' dummy of Ulysses S. Grant's *Personal Memoirs* published by Charles L. Webster & Company founded by Mark Twain. The dummy had been used by canvasser Eliza Geiger of Staten Island, and it included records of her sales and subscribers along with three different, and differently priced, binding specimens. Eliza's equipment may now be viewed at the Library of Congress.

It is a far cry from the domain of the publisher to the battlefield, and a military career is a non-traditional occupation for women whose acceptability remains in dispute. We have welcomed to our shelves three interesting candidates for that profession, each from a different century. In October 1427, at the climax of the Hundred Years War, the Maid of Orleans, assisting the Dauphin, relieved the city from the English. Her deed has captivated historians and fiction writers ever since. In 1560 Jean Louis Micqueau provided an erudite source for Joan of Arc's courageous military command, and any writer recording the great Siege of Orleans had to highlight the young woman's role. Léon Trippault's account of the siege was presumably based upon documents found in Joan's residence, and it pictures the Maid clad in white armor, bestriding a black charger, leading an army of 6000 against the English intruders. Another history of Joan of Arc, published in 1612, was written by a descendant, Jean Hordal, who based his work upon original documents in the Royal Library. Our copy included two full-page plates of the Maid, one on horseback in full armor, the other holding the sword of the realm. In 1427, Joan of Arc played the role of "chef de guerre." Today we are hesitating over the concept of women in the military.

Although our accounts of the seventeenth-century French Amazon Geneviève Prémoy were fictionalized, she did serve as a cavalry officer in the royal dragoons under the name of "Chevalier Baltazar." Her military feats have made for at least two adventure novels, *L'Héroine Travestie* and *Histoire de la Dragone,* but the novels were historical, and their narratives still confirm the capability of the woman soldier.

One of the most intriguing figures of eighteenth-century France was a military hero who was also a diplomat—envoy to the court of Elizabeth of Russia—and a political adventurer. The Chevalier d'Eon de Beaumont was also apparently a highly successful transvestite whose sex posed a mystery to his/her contemporaries. Today he/she is regarded as anatomically male, but from midlife he/she assumed a female identity pursuing non-traditional occupations for women. It was as a woman that Eon appeared in the Russian court, and on the battlefield he/she could be addressed either as Chevalier or as Chevalière. Whether or not Eon de Beaumont strengthens the cause of women in the military, he/she certainly provides a colorful personality in la vie militaire.

The admission of women to military life is patently one of the numerous rights for which feminist advocates have fought and are still fighting. Our early women authors, some of them humanistically educated, most of them skillful and creative in their writings, seldom appealed directly for legal rights to property or fair divorce laws, for suffrage or egalitarianism, or even for the right to a military career. It took other women and other times to urge and advance such rights. It took women whose writings were manifestoes and whose cause was feminism.

Both emancipation and egalitarianism had to begin with education. That was a subject that deeply concerned Mary Astell, dubbed "the first English feminist," author of a *Serious Proposal to the Ladies*. The college for women she envisioned naturally called forth criticism and slander. Attributed to Mary Astell, but in all likelihood by Judith Drake, the *Essay In Defense of the Female Sex* published in 1696 aims frankly "to reduce the Sexes to a Level, and ... to raise Ours to an Equallity ... with the Men." This goal, so devoutly to be wished, is based upon improvements in female education and recommends the study of English rather than Latin and Greek books. Many later writers refused to be swayed by such recommendations, and the subject of woman's education continued to be debated, usually anonymously. *Strictures on Female Education* in 1788 stressed the dangers as well as the inefficiencies of women's boarding schools, while *Sketches of the History ... of the Fair Sex ... By a Friend to the Sex* boldly declared in 1807 that the concept of "female inferiority" led to "the most absurd, unreasonable, and humiliating" notions.

If "female inferiority" precluded women from higher education in the eyes of some male observers, the subject of marriage and divorce stirred up even more debate and disdain. About ten years ago we were able to acquire the following macho but anonymous title, probably the earliest or one of the earliest separate treatises on divorce: *Discovrs Svr Le Divorce Qvi se Fait par L'Adultère, & si'l est permis a l'homme de se remarier*. Writing in 1586, the author considers divorce only on the grounds of adultery and speculates upon whether *man* is entitled to remarry. Despite the exclusionary nature of the title, some slight consideration is given to the entitlement or non-entitlement of women. Nonetheless, divorce—1586 style—surely seems weighted in favor of the male sex.

We were naturally more inclined to acquire pro-women titles, and so we delighted in a few American items on conjugality that favored the role of women. One was the anonymous *American Spectator, or Matrimonial Preceptor,* an anonymous collection of essays on "the Married State ... adapted to the State of Society in the American Republic." Published in Boston in 1797, the work surveyed marriage from matchmaking to conjugal problems. The anonymous author vindicated the female sex, remarking that "in this sequestered happy region" "the rights of women, as well as of men" are acknowledged. The frontispiece shows a conjugal scene at table where the husband stands and the wife is seated.

Nearly a century later, the radical American pamphleteer Ezra Hervey Heywood voiced strong feminist pleas for the unfettered rights of women in marriage or in single blessedness. In *Cupid's Yokes* he delivered so strong a statement on marriage reform that it led to his prosecution for circulating the work through the mails, and to a brief imprisonment.

Of all the rights for which women and their champions fought, none produced a larger body of books and pamphlets than legal and political rights. From the laws of inheritance to the right of suffrage, from a role as citizen to a role as office-holder, women and their male supporters ranged, pleading, orating, writing manifestoes.

Thinking women wished to be heard, wished to make a difference. As early as 1649, Suzanne de Nervèze wrote a Mazarinade—a political pamphlet issued during the tenure of Mazarin, prime minister of France—that agitated for peace in the country. Among the thousands of Mazarinades printed during the struggle known as The Fronde, few indeed were penned by women. This was one of them, and it might have been entitled "A Woman Strikes for Peace."

Prior to the French Revolution women had begun to band together to strike out for causes in which they believed. They began acting as if they had not only a private life but a public life as well. In 1784 the women of Paris addressed a plea to the great French financier Necker, demanding their rights and privileges. Although there were twelve million French women, they stated, they were not consulted by the States General. Listing grievances connected with taxation, the Salic law on dower inheritance, pensions, fashion, the education of children, their *Lettre* to Necker cried out for recognition of the political rights of women.

The voice of women was beginning to resonate in France. On the eve of the French Revolution, the *Très-Humbles Rémontrances des Femmes Françaises* do not read "humbly." Rather, women assert their rights, condemn men's disregard of their views, demand a place in government. Of all the French Revolutionary feminists, perhaps none was more eloquent than Olympe de Gouges, who fought for women's emancipation and the enunciation of their political rights. In a *Séance Royale* of 1789 she boldly asserted that it was "affreux" (horrendous) that women do not have the same advantages as men.

A strong feminist political appeal to participate in the English war against Napoleonic France appeared in the form of a large broadside in 1803. Three months after the outbreak of hostilities, a "Female Subscription" was launched at Lloyd's for money to oppose Napoleon and his threatened invasion of England. In *"An English Woman," To the Women of England* the anonymous author suggested that, by contributing their gold, silver and jewels to the British Treasury, women could participate in the resistance to tyranny and terror. Thus they could also participate in political life.

The French complaint of 1784 that women were not *consulted* by the States General turned five years later into a request that women be *admitted* to the States General. By 1803 English women were enrolling, if not as soldiers on the battlefield, then economically and politically as active participants in a war. The history of women in political life was being impelled forward. The right to vote alone probably resulted in a larger body of ephemeral pamphlets and lengthy tomes than any other political demand by feminists. We assembled a few small collections on woman suffrage, especially on that cause in our own country. One of the most arresting items we acquired was the broadside *Appeal to the Women of the United States by the National Woman Suffrage and Educational Committee* issued in 1871. The *Appeal*, signed by six distinguished feminists including Susan B. Anthony, contained the Declaration and Pledge of the Women of the United States concerning their right to and use of elective franchise. That *Appeal* is surely a landmark in the history of suffrage and hence in the feminist involvement in political activity.

The step from participation in government to holding office in government is a giant step. Our two most dramatic examples of women aiming at high office were both American and most appropriate for us to handle. Victoria Woodhull and Belva Lockwood had been subjects of chapters in Stern's *We the Women: Career Firsts of Nineteenth-Century America,* first published in 1962. The alluringly feminine and staunchly feminist Woodhull presented a *Memorial* before the House Judiciary Committee in 1871, proposing that, if women were citizens, their vote was already guaranteed to them by the Constitution. Suffrage was a right of citizenship. We were delighted to own the pamphlet containing not only the Woodhull *Memorial* but the Majority and Minority House reports on it. Shortly after, the seductive Woodhull acted on her beliefs and campaigned for the presidency of the United States. She was formally nominated by the Equal Rights Party, but unfortunately her campaign was an abortive one since the candidate was forced to spend more time in jail on a charge of libel than on the campaign trail.

If, as Woodhull believed, "to vote, without regard to sex" was a constitutional right, then women were also constitutionally entitled to run for office. America's second woman candidate for the presidency actually did so. Belva Lockwood, a lawyer from upstate New York, defender of the rights of native Americans as well as of women, ran in 1884 and again in 1888. We could not resist a campaign poster addressed to the women of Stonington, Connecticut. The broadside urged the women of Stonington to "throw off the yoke of the oppressor man" and attend a speech by a supporter of Lockwood's election to the "Presidentesscy" of the United States. Lockwood herself would be present, and the occasion would be honored with a triumphal parade and grand banquet. The affair was scheduled for November 5, 1888, the night before election. The next day, despite the hoopla, Benjamin Harrison won the presidency.

The right of suffrage and the right of office-holding, the legal rights, the right to participate in all occupations including the non-traditional, may be summed up in one word, *egalitarianism.* Egalitarianism is implied in all the rights women activists have demanded. Several men champions of women have been aware of this. One of the earliest to engage our attention was the French writer Rustaing de Saint-Jory,

A

VINDICATION

OF THE

RIGHTS OF WOMAN:

WITH

STRICTURES

ON

POLITICAL AND MORAL SUBJECTS.

BY MARY WOLLSTONECRAFT.

LONDON:

PRINTED FOR J. JOHNSON, N° 72, ST. PAUL'S CHURCH YARD.

1792.

First Feminist Literary Landmark

author of a romance entitled *Les Femmes Militaires* published in Paris in 1735. Rustaing's romance is set in a feminist utopia located in America, and its distinctive feature is the absolute parity of men and women in every kind of work and every form of government service.

The great nineteenth-century English political economist John Stuart Mill would have applauded Rustaing's utopian novel. His celebrated book, *The Subjection of Women,* is basically an endorsement of egalitarianism, for in this, his last work, he opposes the legal subordination of one sex to another and pleads for sexual equality. The fact that his stepdaughter had a hand in *The Subjection of Women* simply confirms his appreciation of women.

It took an American writing about the same time as Mill to suggest a syntactical reform to bolster the concept of egalitarianism. George William Curtis, in his speech before the 1867 New York State Constitutional Convention, requested the addition of the pronoun *she* to all occurrences of the pronoun *he* in the state constitution. The speech when printed bore the title *Equal Rights for All.*

For us, there are three women who, not only in their writings but in their lives, seem to personify equal rights for all. In one way or another they illustrate the struggle for legal, personal, political, occupational, and sexual rights that characterize the development of feminism. We buy their writings whenever possible, and we rejoice in their accomplishments.

The first and perhaps the best-known is Mary Wollstonecraft whose *Vindication of the Rights of Woman* is considered the first literary landmark in the feminist movement. It has been analyzed widely and deeply, especially for its condemnation of woman's degradation and its espousal of female education. The *Vindication* exerted influence not only in England but in France where it was translated the year of its original publication—1792. The *Défense des Droits des Femmes* conveyed to readers across the Channel the salutary effects that a feminist revolution could effect, and its message impacted strongly upon a France in revolution.

In Wollstonecraft's *Historical and Moral View of the ... French Revolution,* her feminism is implied. As she unfolded the events in France she unfolded also her own attitudes toward them, seeing the Revolution as "natural consequences of intellectual improvement." Whether she discussed liberty of the press, the destructive influence of commerce, or the progress of reform, she reflected her own opinions and credo—highly intellectual, always egalitarian.

To disseminate foreign ideas in Britain, the English publisher Joseph Johnson assigned translations to Wollstonecraft. One of them was Jacques Necker's *De L'Importance des Opinions Religieuses,* containing the French economist's views on the relation of religion and government. Wollstonecraft's translation, *Of the Importance of Religious Opinions,* was republished in Boston where it proved popular reading for a nation dedicated in some measure to freedom of worship, and receptive to the interpretations of a woman.

Mary Wollstonecraft was not only a translator and author of a great feminist milestone, but a story-teller. Her *Original Stories from Real Life* is a collection that stems from her early experience as governess to Lady Kingsborough's daughters. The stories reflect her attitudes toward women in various roles and mirror her rage at oppression, her desire to ameliorate the ills of society in housing, diet and medical care—not to mention the debasement of women.

Our Wollstonecraft holdings were not complete without the *Memoirs of the Author of a Vindication of the Rights of Woman* by her husband William Godwin. Published in 1798, the year after her death, the *Memoirs* discuss in detail both her attitude toward the French Revolution and the views in *Vindication.* To the *Memoirs* we added a set of Wollstonecraft's *Posthumous Works* published at Godwin's suggestion in four volumes the same year of 1798. Here may be found "The Wrongs of Woman, or Maria"; a fragment on the management of infants; her hints for the second (never published) part of the *Rights of Woman.* In Wollstonecraft's writings as well as in her life, those rights were implicit.

The translator of the French version of Wollstonecraft's *Vindication* remains anonymous. To us it seems quite possible that the translator was our second notable exponent of the rights of women—Helen Maria Williams. Far less well-known than Wollstonecraft, Williams had much in common with her, especially her affiliation with France where she resided for many years. Although Williams was a prolific author, it is her life rather than her writings that proclaims her a liberated woman.

Born in 1762, Helen Maria Williams was an English writer, an early enthusiast for revolutionary France, a femme fatale who lived with but may or may not have married her lover, part owner of his

English Press in Paris, and, like Wollstonecraft, a historian of the French Revolution. At least one copy of her *Poems,* published in London in 1786, was subscribed for by John Hurford Stone who would become founder of the English Press in Paris as well as the poet's lover. Williams' initial enthusiasm for French Revolutionary principles when "the love of liberty… pervaded all ranks of the people" is manifest in her early *Letters* on the French Revolution. As France moved from "the love of liberty" to a reliance on terror, Williams' attitude changed. Both she and John Hurford Stone were confined in Luxembourg prison in October 1793, and her *Letters* on events during the tyranny of Robespierre demonstrate her altered reaction. The "knife of the guillotine suspended" over her, she fled to Switzerland where she received news of the fall of Robespierre, and her series of *Letters* weaves a rich tapestry of France by an eye-witness who was also a feminist. The "wreck of civil liberty," the persecution of Protestants in France, French censorship, intrigue and repression all color her observations as she chronicles the diminution of revolutionary romance and ardor. Williams lived her life exactly as she wished— abroad, in the company of her lover, helping him maintain his press, viewing the changing political life around her as a forthright feminist witness. Williams did not write a *Vindication* of woman—she lived the rights of women.

Our pioneer American feminist did both. Margaret Fuller's personal life embodied women's rights; her *Woman in the Nineteenth Century* was their clarion call. In 1845 her masterpiece struck out for egalitarianism in all its aspects, from the legal and political rights of women to their pursuit of non-traditional vocations. ("Let them be sea-captains, if you will.") Fuller was especially close to our hearts not only because of her credo, but because she had been the subject of Stern's first biography in 1942.

Hence, when we found an autograph letter of 1849 that introduced and described Margaret Fuller, we reveled in it. The letter, unknown and unpublished, was written in Italian by one Italian poet, Giovanni Berchet, to another, Giovanni Count Marchetti. Dated from Florence, 30 June, while Fuller was still abroad, the letter describes her as a "Letterata Americana," an American writer of the finest sentiments, whose acute intellect perceives men and events with judgment and benevolence. She is both vivacious and cordial, and Giovanni Berchet hopes that the Dante scholar Count Marchetti will extend to her his warm friendship. The letter not only epitomized Fuller's nature but cast light upon the recognition she enjoyed in Italy and her place among its poets and intellectuals. The envelope in which Berchet had placed it was present, as well as the endorsement in Margaret Fuller's hand. She had carried the letter with her, and it still breathed her essence. The following year she would leave Italy with her husband and her son, and all would perish in the shipwreck of the barque *Elisabeth*.

Male recognition of women scholars—the Margaret Fullers of history—was far less prevalent than male elevation of woman as chaste and innocent symbol. On our shelves such recognition began with Boccaccio, whose *De Claris Mulieribus* included accounts of productive and learned Renaissance women. Along with the virtuous and pious women in his *Triomphe Des Dames* of 1599, Pierre de Brinon saw fit to discuss scholarly women. Early in the seventeenth century, an Italian, Ribera, published a biographical dictionary of women arranged according to their careers in science and medicine, astrology and painting, and even the military life. By the end of the seventeenth century, *A Dialogue Concerning Women* by an English critic William Walsh discusses a "Library of Women, Illustrious for their Writings"—surely one of the earliest attempts to assemble a library of books by women. Among them Walsh cites Anna Maria Schurman, "who was indeed a Library her self," as well as Falconia Proba, Thomas More's learned daughters, and Mademoiselle Scudéry. The *Dialogue* contains a preface by John Dryden who finds "in this Age... more Heroines than Heroes."

By the eighteenth century, sections concerned with women scholars appeared frequently in books on women. In his *Essai sur Le Caractère ... Des Femmes,* Antoine Léonard Thomas cites numerous feminist bibliographical references. Antoine de Rivarol in his 1789 *Petit Almanach de nos Grandes Femmes* provides a virtual feminist Who's Who, a biographical dictionary of women achievers: artists and performers, writers, translators, and historians. Rosa Califronia, in her *Breve Difesa dei Diritti Delle Donne* of 1794 *(Brief Defense of the Rights of Women)* not only upholds the rights of her sex but includes a remarkable bibliographical checklist of writings between the sixteenth and eighteenth centuries in support of women. Her work is, in effect, an Italian feminist manifesto based upon bibliographical learning—surely a forerunner of Margaret Fuller's *Woman in the Nineteenth Century.*

A lecture was delivered in Albany, New York, in 1837, giving *Suggestions on the Best Mode of Promoting Civilization and Improvement; or, The Influence of Woman on the Social State.* In it, the speaker, one Samuel Young, summed up as he promoted egalitarianism and the rights of women. In addition, he related the feminist cause to the amelioration of society and in so doing he foreshadowed the question that Bronson Alcott would ask a few decades later in a letter to Lucy Stone: "Where women—the best women, lead is it unsafe for any to follow?... who is the leader? Is it woman?" Such concepts point to egalitarianism and beyond, where the right to participate in government is joined by the right of leadership in government. In Albany in 1837, Samuel Young uttered a pregnant phrase when he painted the "splendid coruscations of female genius." Those coruscations that flickered so long ago now light the sky.

IO.REVCHLIN PHORCENS.DOCTOR
IVRIS. COMES PALATINVS LATE
RANVS.SICAMBRORVM LEGISTACI
TVS ET SVEVIAE TRIVMVIR.FRIDE
RICO .III.IMP.RO.INSIGNIS.

VIVAT CAPNION FOELIX
V.G·D·

ARACAP

NIONIS

Hebrew Scholarship 1506

VIII
The Jews

Our strong interest in feminist books stems in part from the fact that we are women. In the same way, we are drawn to books on the Jews because we are Jews. But there are other potent reasons as well. The Jews, though an extremely small minority, have given rise to a great and enormously influential majority called Christianity, rulers now of a good part of the world. This extraordinary circumstance has resulted in all sorts of conditions and problems, prejudices and opinions, philosophies and cataclysmic events—as well as a great and fascinating literature. Whenever we can, we add to our historical store by purchasing the known and unknown treasures of Judaica.

During a buying trip abroad in the 60s, we acquired a remarkable copy of one of those remarkable treasures. In April 1506, the printer Anshelm of Pforzheim, Germany, used three different type fonts to produce a milestone in the history of Jewish scholarship. Two fonts were Hebrew, for the book by the distinguished German scholar Johann Reuchlin was "the first important grammar" of the Hebrew language. A result in part of Reuchlin's own great learning, and in part of his desire to disseminate the study of Hebrew in Germany, the *De Rvdimentis Hebraicis Liber Primvs* set high standards in early Hebrew language scholarship. It also, in time, involved its renowned author in a controversy with the antisemitic scholar Pfefferkorn, that added fuel to the fire of the Reformation. Our copy of that seminal work had belonged to the author's brother Dionysius Reuchlin, who inserted by hand a brief curriculum vitae of the author from his birth in 1455 to his death in 1522: "Requiescat cum Beatis In pace."

Before resting in peace with the blessed, Johann Reuchlin took time to write other works of Judaic and Hebraic interest that found their way to our shelves. What did he choose to write about the Jews, this most eminent of the Christian Judaic scholars of the Renaissance who taught Greek and Hebrew at Tübingen? When Pfefferkorn accused him of heresy for his support of Hebrew studies, and Hoogstraten, prior of the Dominicans of Cologne, encouraged the destruction of Hebrew books, Reuchlin replied with a *Defensio*—less a defense of himself than a defense of the study of Hebrew language and literature. Reuchlin continued his investigation of both, and his *De Accentibvs et Orthographia Lingvae Hebraicae* of 1518 found space in its investigation of Hebrew syllabication for twelve pages of music including an ancient synagogue chant for four voices. Our copy had been owned by a noted sixteenth-century French humanist who was also a Hebraist, Guillaume Postel.

It was a distinguished group of Renaissance scholars who chronicled for us the early development of Hebrew studies. The name of Reuchlin was united with that of "the first printer of Hebrew books in Venice," Daniel Bomberg, in the 1522 edition of the *Hagiographa*. Along with Proverbs, Song of Songs, and Ecclesiastes, the *Hagiographa* included a letter of February 1522 from Bomberg to Reuchlin, referring to the former's work on the Talmud. The tiny volume—a 16mo—was cased in a beautiful Grolieresque binding, and over the centuries it passed through many hands. Leaving Bomberg's Venetian press, it was acquired in 1540—as an autograph inscription told us—by Leger Duchesne ("Lud. Querculus"), a French scholar-poet who taught at the Collège de France. More than four centuries later, it was purchased by us, and we passed it on to an ardent Hebraic bibliophile, Irving Levitas of Yonkers, New York.

Many of our Renaissance pioneers in Hebrew scholarship concerned themselves with Hebrew as a language. In 1520, the German Johann Boechenstein published an *Introdvctio* to Hebrew in which he presented the Hebrew Alphabet based on the first Hebrew alphabet printed by Aldus Manutius, along with the Lord's Prayer and the Hail Mary in Hebrew. The eminent Sebastian Münster, who taught Hebrew theology at Basle, and had been the pupil of Elijah Levitas (ancestor of Irving Levitas?), produced a Hebrew grammar that became a popular school manual.

Like Sebastian Münster, the German humanist Paul Fagius learned Hebrew from Elijah Levitas, and around 1540 set up a press at Isny in the Swiss canton of Allgau for the dissemination of Hebrew literature. There he published his own translations and commentaries on original Hebrew texts of festival prayers, the ethical maxims of the *Pirke Abot,* and the proverbs and fables of the *Alphabet of Ben Sira.* Because of his own religious beliefs, Fagius would flee to England where he would be appointed reader in Hebrew at the University of Cambridge. Hebrew scholarship had begun its wide dissemination.

It was, indeed, a member of the London Stationers Company who had a hand in the spread of Hebrew scholarship in Britain. The printer

Richard Jugge suggested to Peter Morwen the desirability of translating into English a tenth-century Hebrew compilation attributed to Joseph ben Gorion. The result was *A compendious and most marveilous Historie of the latter tymes of the Iewes common weale,* published by Jugge for the third time in 1567. This popular chronicle of Jewish history from Adam to the Age of Titus circulated widely in England and was frequently reprinted. Perhaps it became one small link in the long chain that would lead eventually to the readmission of Jews into England.

The Jews had been expelled from England by a decree promulgated in 1290 by King Edward I. Through the long centuries between their expulsion and their readmission, the work of Christian champions of Jews and their cultural history was offset by the work of Christian adversaries of the Jews. Although the testimony to antisemitism far outweighs the testimony to prosemitism, we were understandably never eager to admit antisemitic writings to our holdings. Nonetheless, a few examples strayed in, infamous reminders of persecution and its destructive power.

When it came to the Jews, Martin Luther was less the great Reformer than the great antagonist. Jesus Christ, he conceded, had been born a Jew, but had redeemed himself from that birthright through his deeds and thoughts. Luther's comments on the subject were expressed in his *Das Jhesus Christus ain geborner Jude sey* of 1523. As for the Jews themselves, one of Luther's most powerful sermons, delivered in 1520 on the horrors of usury, was also directed against Jewish practitioners of usury. That the practice had been virtually forced upon the Jews is not considered; usury is denounced as a baleful influence on the German nation, and the sermon is not only a condemnation of avarice and profiteering but a violent expression of antisemitism.

In its attitude toward Jews, the Catholic Church was one with the Reformers. In a collection of Papal Bulls we acquired from a Bolognese dealer during a buying trip in the 60s, we found testimony to that attitude. The *Confirmatio Capitulorum sup[er] reformatione Bancheriorum Haebreorum,* promulgated by Pope Pius IV in 1565, placed tight controls upon the Jewish bankers of Rome, their interest rates, bookkeeping and relations with Christian creditors. Three years later, the new pope, Pius V, went further. An earlier Pope—Paul IV—had already restricted the Jews of Rome to a ghetto and limited their professional activity. Now, in 1568, Pius V expelled the Jews from many of the Papal States, and among the charges against them he cited mystical incantation, association with the devil, and the practice of usury.

The passage of time seems to have had little effect upon anti-semitism. Certainly we found copious testimony of its continuance in the seventeenth century. The city fathers and guilds of Frankfurt banned the "useless Jewish rabble" who congregated at the Corn-market on Sundays and whose responsibility for all municipal wrongs is still evidenced in a pamphlet, *Copia ... und Protestation.*

France was in accord with Germany on the subject of the Jews. The *Lettres Patentes* of 1615 addressed to all Jews and practitioners of Judaism by Louis XIII advised them that, within a month after the edict's publication, and under pain of death and confiscation of property, Jews must leave the kingdom.

Most of our antisemitic testimonials single out the economic role of the Jew for special vituperation: usurious rates, coin clipping, terms of money-lending. Although the Jews survived the accusations, the expulsions, some of them did not survive as Jews. We had, for example, an eighteenth-century *Très-Humble Supplique* in which five thousand Jews of Poland and Hungary, Moldavia, Wallachia and Turkey, having lived through the barbarities of eastern Europe, appealed for conversion and baptism into Roman Christianity. The conversion of banished and dispersed Jews was one device for survival.

One of the best-known examples of nineteenth-century anti-semitism has become known as the Dreyfus Affair: the case in which the French Jewish Captain Alfred Dreyfus was falsely charged with spying in 1894 and was condemned to Devils Island. Three years later, the actual criminal Esterhazy was accused of forgery and tried by court-martial, but Esterhazy, a non-Jew, was acquitted. It was not until the celebrated French novelist and journalist Emile Zola took on the defense of Captain Dreyfus that justice was eventually done. It was Zola who challenged the government to give Dreyfus a hearing, and the following year the case was taken up by Clemenceau. Lasting a dozen years (not till 1906 was Dreyfus finally restored to the army), the Affair gave rise to a library of printed records and opinions. One of our favorites is Zola's letter pleading for justice on behalf of a French Jew. Entitled *Humanité-Verité-Justice. L'Affaire Drefus,* it was issued in Paris in 1897 and bound in its original printed wrappers. Zola pleaded for humanity, truth and justice. Prosemitism was the antiphonal response to antisemitism.

From time to time, scattered protests against antisemitic attitudes reached our desks from various countries. An early eighteenth-century study of the legal rights of Italian Jews by Sessa, a jurist from Turin, accepted their position in business and their entitlements in inheritance cases, lawsuits, marriage contracts, as well as in their relations with the state. A German professor of law at the University of Altdorf, Johann Beck, published a collection of the laws controlling Jewish life from birth to death. His *Tractatus De Juribus Judaeorum, von Recht der Juden* of 1731 had a compartmental frontispiece illustrating those legal phases: a bride, Jewish merchants, the deathbed signing of a Will with lawyers present.

English support for the Jews, judging from our holdings, went beyond concentration upon law to involvement with their history and status as British citizens. One of the most interesting of our books on the subject was *A Comparison Betvveene the Dayes of Pvrim and that of the Powder Treason* of 1626, in which the author—George Hakewill—compared the Feast of Purim with the threat of the gunpowder treason. Demonstrating uncommon sympathy for the plight of the Jews, the author viewed them as victims of "Haman's bloudy design for their vtter extirpation."

Descendants of the victims of Haman, migrating to England in the mid-eighteenth century, hoped of course for citizenship. In due course, Parliament debated a "Bill to Permit Persons professing the Jewish Religion to be Naturalized," and the terms of the Bill were vehemently argued back and forth by prosemites and antisemites. Adopted in 1753, the Bill would be repealed the following year! We especially applauded the vindication of the Jews as British citizens by "Philo-Patriae," because his arguments centered precisely on the very subject that had kindled so much antisemitism—the economic position of the Jews. "Philo-Patriae" believed that the economic value of the Jews to England, their usefulness in trade, their influence on increased balance of profits, strongly favored the naturalization of Jews in Britain.

Implicit in prosemitic writings is the antisemitism that triggered it. We found the two bound together in a single volume: Joseph Priestley's *Letters to the Jews* and David Levi's *Letters to Dr. Priestley.* The great British scientist and philosopher Joseph Priestley, discussing the privileges and dispersed state of the Jews, suggested in his *Letters* that Jews either compromise with Christians or convert. To this proposal David Levi replied, analyzing Priestley's fallacies, commenting on the dispersion of the Jews, comparing Moses with Christ, affirming the god-given nature of the Jewish religion, and demanding a retraction from Priestley. Our copy of this antiphon was in the first American edition of 1794, having been published in New York by that city's "first Jewish Bookseller," Benjamin Gomez.

Most of the prosemitic books and pamphlets that we acquired dated from the latter part of the eighteenth century and hailed from France. Like England's "Philo-Patriae," who applauded the role of Jews in trade, the French Jew, Israel Bernard de Vallabregue, wrote an anonymous *Lettre* in 1768, condemning the opposition of the guilds to French Jews, and citing their expertise in business as a prime reason for their acceptance. Around the same time, a volume entitled *Lettres de Quelques Juifs Portugais et Allemands,* addressed to M. de Voltaire, appeared anonymously. Actually it had been written by a French controversialist, Antoine Guénée, to expose the errors and sarcasms in Voltaire's references to the Jews. Voltaire, champion of the beleaguered French Protestant Jean Calas, author of the *Treatise on Toleration,* castigator of religious prejudice, had apparently not extended his liberalism to the Jews. Monsieur Guénée, discussing Jewish thought and history, science and language, took pains to set the matter straight.

In large measure, it was the French Revolution that accomplished this by applying the Declaration of the Rights of Man to the Rights of the Jews. Even before the Revolution, in 1788, there are hints of such an endeavor in a *Dissertation* on the question of whether there are means of making the Jews happier and more useful in France. Written by Thiery, a lawyer of Nancy, the volume discusses the Jews of the provinces and points out especially the necessity of Jewish participation in communal activity. An author's presentation copy of this plea for political and judicial equality for Jews left our premises for the Lilly Library of Indiana University.

Jewish demand for equal rights accelerated. Our *Mémoire Pour Les Juifs de Luneville et de Sarguemines* reminded the National Assembly that Jews must not be excluded from "Egalité." Abbé Henri Grégoire, the great French Revolutionary theorist and defender of minorities, produced in his *Essai sur la régénération physique … et politique des Juifs* a brilliant manifesto for the recognition and full participation in affairs of state of all Jews.

On January 28, 1790, notice was taken. A *Pétition Des Juifs* addressed to the National Assembly had appealed for equality in civic status. Now the Portuguese Jews of Bayonne and Bordeaux were successful, and were granted their emancipation—a short step in a long direction. As the momentous months of 1790 succeeded each other, further appeals were made, and the French Revolution pamphlets on the status of the Jews mounted up, among them Louis XVI's *Lettres Patentes* relating to admission to French citizenship of the Portuguese Jews of Bayonne and Bordeaux. The king's *Proclamation* on the National Assembly's decree concerning the Jews accepted the legislation of the Assembly in two landmark pages. Another royal *Lettres-Patentes* specified required conditions for the exercise by Jews of the rights of citizenship. Still another abolished taxes levied against Jews for their domiciles and protection.

The great majority of Jews—some 20,000—resided in 1790 in Alsace. Delegate Duport had forced the question of freedom for Alsatian Jews before the National Assembly, and they themselves had circulated an *Adresse des Juifs Alsaciens au Peuple d'Alsace* in 1790 and forwarded their appeal to Mendelssohn. The emancipation of the Jews of Alsace was accomplished, and on September 27, 1791, the emancipation of all Jews, so long and frequently appealed for and debated, became final and official. At long last, and "for the first time in the history of modern Europe, the Jews were formally admitted equal citizens of the country of their birth." Our *Recueil de Pièces Relatives A L'Admission des Juifs à L'Etat Civil* includes a discourse delivered by a lawyer, Godard, at the January 28, 1790 meeting of the National Assembly. In it the delegate cites the contributions of Jews to French culture and scholarship as well as to French patriotism. The *Recueil*, enriched with documentary material, discourses and opinions, is a comprehensive milestone in the long struggle for the Egalité of Jews that crowned—for a time—the ever-recurrent conflict between antisemitism and prosemitism.

Throughout the course of that unceasing antiphon, the scholars—non-Jewish and Jewish—were at work, seeking objectivity in their presentation of Jewish history.

Pioneer Renaissance Jewish scholarship was followed, according to the evidence that passed through our hands, by detailed investigations of Jewish laws, language and history. Studies of those subjects by non-Jews seem to have been untinged by prejudice and motivated by a desire to arrive at the truth about an ancient people. Seventeenth-century Scottish scholars—John Row, William Robertson—compiled Hebrew grammars and word books with linguistic commentaries for the elucidation of students. Etienne Morin, who taught oriental languages at the University of Amsterdam, attempted to prove that the Hebrew language had been communicated to Adam by God. Even the Vatican seemed to accept this hypothesis. The Roman Church had established its Congregation for the Propaganda of the Faith to proselytize in newly discovered lands. In 1771 the Congregation's press—a polyglot printing house—used its fonts of exotic type to export Hebrew to the heathen, and issued an *Alphabetum Hebraicum* including not only the editor's foreword but the Lord's Prayer. A few years later, the Christian Hebraist De Rossi, professor of oriental languages at Parma, wrote a disquisition on Hebrew typography. For this he provided a list of fifty Hebrew books published between 1477 and 1500, and so produced in his *De Hebraicae Typographiae Origine ... Disquisitio* one of the early works in systematic Hebraic-Judaic bibliography. By the nineteenth century, one scholar at least—Henry Craik—based his Hebrew manual on the methods of the Swiss educational reformer Pestalozzi. Pestalozzi had based *his* methods on Rousseau's *Emile,* and so Craik's *Easy Introduction to the Hebrew Language on the Principles of Pestalozzi* was an attempt to teach Hebrew by a return to nature!

Hebrew law attracted scholars too. An expert in ancient tongues, L'Empereur ab Obwyck, professor of Hebrew at the University of Leyden, compiled a study of Hebrew business law, the nature of exchange, selling, the validity of contracts, that proved useful and popular in the large Dutch Jewish ghetto. Far more interesting was an eighteenth-century *Recueil,* an anonymous collection on a Judaic legal question that did not remain long on our shelves. One of the most intriguing compendiums relating to the status of Jewish women and wives, the work focuses upon a single legal case, that of an Alsatian Jew with a Jewish wife who in 1752 went to Paris, converted to Catholicism, and changed his name. His wife refused either to abandon her faith or to cohabit with her husband. When the husband determined to marry a Catholic, notwithstanding his legitimate wife's position, the pleas, memoirs and appeals accumulated and our *Recueil* was published. Here was a case that cast light upon the power and the plight of a Jewish wife who refused to abandon her religion, a case that not only publicized but helped shape Jewish law.

The majority of our Hebraic books written by non-Jews are concerned with various phases of Jewish history. The German scholar Paul Eber traced the annals of Jews from their return from the Babylonian exile to the last sack of Jerusalem. A compatriot of Eber concentrated upon the life of Queen Esther for his Göttingen dissertation. By 1736, when he presented his thesis, the inconsistencies and improbabilities of her story had come to be questioned, and the Göttingen scholar, supplying a learned array of sources and annotations, elucidated the life of the Jewish woman Esther who foiled a plot to massacre the Jews.

From Queen Esther to the Sephardic tribes in the Berber states, Judaic history elicited the attention of non-Jewish scholars. Along with the history of the Jews, they considered and dissected the Mosaic Code, Jewish theocracy, the Talmud and the Cabbala, rabbinical traditions, Jewish rites and festivals, calendar and forms of prayer, the Messiah. Fascination with Judaica was not confined to the continent of Europe. When the eighteenth-century English publisher Nathaniel Crouch compiled *A Journey to Jerusalem,* he included a lengthy section on the Jews in America from the Spanish West Indies to Mexico and conjectured that the "first inhabitants of America were the ten tribes of the Israelites." The American Jacob Green, pastor of the Presbyterian church in Morris County, New Jersey, a polymath who practiced physic, drafted wills, taught Latin, and ran a grist-mill and a distillery, wrote a fascinating study in 1768: *An Inquiry into The Constitution and Discipline of the Jewish Church.* In it he explored the sacramentarian controversy and the concept of grace, and to expound those issues, analyzed Jewish rites and practices, faith and dogma.

By the nineteenth century, a society was established by American non-Jews to aid, and if possible to convert, the Jews of New York. This American Society for Meliorating the Condition of the Jews issued annual sermons and reports. In one of them we found insightful remarks on Jewish trade and education, as well as a sermon by clergyman William Sprague on the history and calamities of the Jews. Christian history was sometimes used to provide understanding of Jewish history, as when Joseph Turner in *The True Israel* analyzed the Epistle of Paul to the Romans to explain the nature of the Jew, his faith in the Messiah, the Mosaic economy, the tribes of Israel, the Jews as God's chosen people. Turner's opinions were published in 1850 in Hartford where a large group of Jews were settling after the Revolution of 1848 in Germany.

מקוה ישראל

Hoc est,

S P E S

ISRAELIS.

Authore

Menasseh Ben Israel

Theologo & Philosopho Hebræo.

Menasseh ben israel

AMSTELODAMI

ANNO 1650.

The Dream of Judaism

THE

Hope of Israel:

Written

By *MENASSEH BEN ISRAEL,*
An Hebrew Divine, and
Philosopher.

Newly extant, and Printed at *Am-*
sterdam, and Dedicated by the Author, to
the High Court the Parliament of *England,*
and to the Councell of State.

Whereunto are added
Some Discourses upon the point of the
Conversion of the Jewes :

By MOSES WALL.

The second Edition Corrected and amended.

LONDON Printed by *R.I.* for *Livewell Chap-*
man at the Crown in Popes-Head Alley
1 6 5 1.

The Dream of Judaism

Along with non-Jewish historians of Judaica and Hebraica, Jewish scholars expanded the horizons of knowledge about the Jews. Undoubtedly they too sought objectivity in their approach to the subject. If that objectivity was not always achieved, it was because, threaded through their commentaries, there sometimes glimmered what had come to be called the Hope of Israel.

The early chronicles of Jewish history that passed to and from our hands always seemed to us to be more than chronicles. Their writers interwove through their investigations their concepts of Judaism and of Jewish philosophy. Recording his history of the Jewish Wars, Josephus, for example, included also his observations about the life of the Jews, their wanderings, their prophets, their merchants and their teachers. Having spent three years in the desert, he could identify with, as he animated, the experiences of his countrymen.

Most of our early works on Judaism by Jewish writers were basically not histories at all but disquisitions on Jewish thought and philosophy. The tenth-century Egyptian Saadias Gaon ben Joseph produced a collection of articles of faith concerned with redemption and deliverance, two subjects in which most Jews were well versed. Saadias' work, opposing the excesses of the mystics and attempting a natural interpretation of Scripture, would eventually influence Maimonides and help lay the foundations of a Jewish philosophy. Our copy of Saadias' *Scepher Aemvnot* was most appropriately printed by the Jewish leader, printer and philosopher Menasseh ben Israel in 1647 at his own press, the first Hebrew press in Amsterdam.

Two centuries after Saadias, the distinguished Hebrew grammarian David Kimhi extended Scriptural understanding with his *Commentaries on the Prophets.* In the sixteenth century his interpretations were translated into Latin by Oxford's professor of Hebrew, Thomas Neal, who dedicated his translation to the English legate at Rome, Cardinal Pole. And so these twelfth-century *Commentaries on the Prophets* of Judaism were introduced to Elizabethan England and, in a way, endorsed by Rome.

In Judaic annals, one commentary always leads to another. Don Isaac Abrabanel, who led the Jews of Spain into exile in 1492, had more to say on the subject of the prophets and said it in his *Peirush Al Neviin Achronim.* We found a copy of the commentary published in Amsterdam in 1641, but without the name of the publisher. We learned that a 1652 catalogue of books printed and sold in the shop of "ben Israel" listed "Abarbanel sobre Profetas" along with several works by Menasseh ben

Israel. We put two and two together, and claimed as a strong probability that Abrabanel's Scriptural observations had issued from Menasseh ben Israel's Hebrew Press in Amsterdam.

So many of our Jewish interpretations of Judaism had no geographical bounds. Unlike the Jews confined to ghettos, these works transcended the limitations of space. The first Hebrew catechism was compiled by Abraham Jaghel, a sixteenth-century rabbi of Sicily. Our version of 1679 was translated from Hebrew into Latin by Louis de Veiel, a French orientalist, and the French orientalist was a resident of London.

The maxims and proverbs of early rabbis and rabbinical commentators provided likely sources for scholarly texts by Jews. One that we found especially interesting was a French translation, *Les Sentences et Proverbes des Anciens Rabins* by a savant and rabbi. Born Mardokhai, the translator converted to Christianity, and taught Hebrew in Paris and at the Collège de France. His name became Philippe d'Aquin or Aquino. He had not, however, forgotten his origins.

In another French version, we handled the *Cérémonies et Coustumes … Parmy Les Juifs* by the late Renaissance Venetian rabbi Leone of Modena, who has been described as "an infant prodigy and hoary prodigal." His work on Jewish social customs is a mine of information on family relations, business interests, education, religious rites, and Christian contacts.

It was yet another rabbi, the Moroccan Marochitanus Samuel, who wrote in Arabic a work on the coming of the Jewish Messiah. Our Latin translation was published in Strasbourg in 1523. Its title-page was printed within an extraordinary woodcut border depicting God above surrounded by Saints Peter and Paul, four Apostles, and below, Mercury and Minerva. The Messianic hope is the golden thread that has gleamed through centuries of despair and desperation for many Jews, the vision too of a Jewish homeland in a regenerated world.

Perhaps no Jewish scholar represents the Hope of Israel better than the author of *The Hope of Israel*. Besides being a Jewish leader, printer, thinker, Menasseh ben Israel, who lived between 1604 and 1657, was truly modern in his scholarship. His purpose was to bring learning "within the grasp of the ordinary man" and to extend it beyond the confines of Jews "for the information of the outside world."

We buy Menasseh ben Israel whenever we can. During the 1960s and 1970s we were especially successful in such acquisitions, and were able to assemble a representative collection of his writings, nearly all of them printed by himself at the Hebrew press in Amsterdam which he established in 1626. The earliest Menasseh imprint we acquired was his *Conciliator,* his attempt to reconcile the apparent discrepancies in the books of the Old Testament, surely an indication of his modern approach to learning. Our next Menasseh was the first of his philosophical works, in first edition of 1635: his treatise on the thirty problems of creation. With this was bound a copy of Menasseh's important study on resurrection, affirmatively grappling with concepts of the soul's immortality and the future state of man. Needless to say, this would be placed on the Index. In 1639, philosophizing on the nature of man, Menasseh published his study on the length of man's life—was this predetermined or changeable?—and, three years later, his *Dissertation* on human weakness and divine assistance in good work.

Besides founding the first Hebrew press in Amsterdam, besides writing books on Judaism that breathe modernity, Menasseh ben Israel was the chief advocate for the readmission of Jews to England under the Commonwealth, and virtual founder of the Anglo-Jewish community. His Amsterdam press issued in 1650 his most significant work, his *Spes Israelis,* his *Hope of Israel,* in which he urged that Jews be readmitted to the country whence they had been expelled in 1290. To accomplish that purpose, Menasseh visited England and had an audience with Cromwell. Meanwhile, in 1651, the *Spes Israelis* was translated into *The Hope of Israel,* and published by a like-minded London publisher, Livewell Chapman, who shared the author's Messianic ideology.

Though resettlement of the Jews in England was not officially accomplished, surely Menasseh led the way to that eventual accomplishment. It was one of several aspirations for Israel that he envisioned, and a collection of his writings is a reminder both of those hopes and of the despairs that motivated them.

Suitable companions for Menasseh emerged for us in the eighteenth century: Moses Mendelssohn with his *Jerusalem,* his mighty vindication of Judaism, upholding the ideals of tolerance and the equality of man; and Mirabeau's *Sur Moses Mendelssohn, sur la Réforme Politique Des Juifs,* on the political reform of the Jews, discussing the Jews of France and Russia, Spain and Holland, their persecution and their usefulness. Mirabeau was not a Jew, but he was a frequent visitor in the salons of

Henrietta Herz and Mendelssohn's daughters; he was also a friend of Jews and a champion of their emancipation.

Jews have been the objects of antisemitism, the subjects of pros-emitism. They have provided topics for historical investigations by non-Jews and philosophical disquisitions by Jews. They have also—despite the First Commandment—supplied material, not for graven images, but for emblems and graphic representations in a variety of fascinating books.

One of them is an oration delivered in 1520 by a Roman citizen, Vitalis, to the recently crowned monarch of the Spanish and Hapsburg dominions, Charles V. The eulogist urges the new emperor to take up arms against the Turks; he also alludes to "the gold and silver of the Indies," "the colonies in the ocean," thus giving Turkish and American interest to what would appear to be merely a routine speech. In addition, and most pertinently, this panegyric is adorned with a full-page woodcut on the title-page depicting a seven-branched candlestick, a Menorah. To find anything where it does not seem to belong is always a source of excitement. To find the image of a Jewish artifact on the title-page of a speech in praise of Charles V is, to say the least, mind-boggling. Probably it was not the orator but the publisher, Guileretus of Rome, who was responsible for its presence here. But why did he include it? Guileretus had issued papal Bulls, some of them directed against the Jews. Had he learned about the Menorah in that connection? Was he reminding his readership that the Jews were also part of the Holy Roman Empire?

A less obvious Jewish association appears on two large maps or plans of the city of Cremona illustrating a magnificent Renaissance vol-ume by Antonio Campo: *Cremona Fedelissima Citta*. The folio is enriched with many plates, one of them depicting Leonardo da Vinci's portrait of Maximilian Sforza, the original of which has been lost. Along with portraits of contemporary notables and engravings of the Duomo, Baptistry and Campanile, this superb tribute to Cremona offers a more or less hidden Judaicum. On a large folding map of Cremona and a map of the surroundings appear the words: "David De Lavde Hebrevs Cremone Incidi." Whatever else the Hebrew David accomplished, he was probably the first Jewish engraver responsible for the execution of a map. We once had a copy of Campo's *Cremona* that had been owned by Henry Howard, First Earl of Northampton, son of the Earl of Surrey, who traveled abroad in 1585 when the work was published. We wonder if he knew about the role of David Hebrevs in the volume—or if he cared.

More obvious and far more curious is the Jewish portraiture found in a *Gründliche Relation Von einem Juden ausz Jerusalem mit Nahmen Ahasuerus* written by a Westphalian scholar in 1634. In this extraordinary *Relation* the author asserts that, according to recent research, a Jewish shoemaker named Ahasuerus witnessed the Crucifixion scene. The large woodcut on the title-page depicts the scene and, towering over it, the Jewish shoemaker Ahasuerus.

It is not surprising to find in a *Guide Ou nouvelle Déscription D'Amsterdam* of 1720, illustrated with twenty folding plates, a fine rendition of the great Portuguese Synagogue. And in a mid-eighteenth-century volume of illustrations for Leone of Modena's work on ceremonies we would expect to find in the series of twelve Judaic plates engraved after the designs of Bernard Picart, representations of the Feast of Passover, nuptial ceremonies, costumes, ritual instruments, as well as the Portuguese Synagogues in The Hague and Amsterdam.

In many of the books we have bought and sold, Jews have sat for their portraits. Along with their portraits, their problems and their hopes recur: the persecutions, expulsions and torments they have been subjected to, the aspirations for which they have dreamed.

In 1751 an unknown author penned a book of *Réflexions Décisives sur le Judaisme,* but his reflections were anything but decisive. Why, he asked, if the Jews know the true God, have they been victims of persecution? Why does their true God permit erring non-Jews to prevail? The author does not answer his question. A comedy by the English dramatist Richard Cumberland produced in 1795 is entitled *The Jew; or, Benevolent Hebrew.* Its hero is Sheva, a rich Jewish merchant who masks his many charities and plans to bequeathe his wealth "to a charitable heir, and build my hospital in the human heart." In his heart Sheva knows that, as a Jew, he is maligned as "Shylock," and he knows too that "we have no abiding place on earth."

The statesman Benjamin Disraeli, a baptised Jew, was raised to high place in England, but nonetheless was reminded by his peers of his Jewish origins. His reply was memorable: "Yes," he agreed. "I am a Jew. And when the ancestors of the right honorable gentlemen were brutal savages on an unknown island, mine were priests in the Temple of

Solomon." The Temple of Solomon was built on Mount Zion in Jerusalem about one thousand years before the birth of Christ. It was Jerusalem to which Jewish victims of Diaspora and prejudice aspired.

We have told the story elsewhere of our finding Theodore Herzl's *Iudenstaat* in first Hebrew edition of 1896 on the eve of Rosh Ha-Shana in the Alesia section of Paris.* We shall not tell the story again. Yet the *Iudenstaat,* the trumpet of Zionism—the plea for a Jewish homeland— epitomizes so well one hope of Israel that it forms a fitting end to this chapter. Herzl's dream—Israel's hope—was realized only in 1948, after the word *Holocaust* had taken on its most destructive and direful connotations. A half-century later, when we turn the pages of *Der Iudenstaat,* and of many of the other books that have come our way, we marshal our thoughts on horror and hope, on the power of destruction and the nature of indestructibility, on death and survival.

---

* In Leona Rostenberg and Madeleine B. Stern, *Connections: Our Selves—Our Books* (Santa Monica: Modoc Press, 1994) pp. 110-112.

IX
The Blacks

The slavery of women, deplored so vehemently by nineteenth-century feminists, was generally attributed and confined to the not-so-holy state of matrimony in which man was master. The enslavement of the Jews during the Babylonian captivity did not persist for centuries and did not basically undermine their identity or their creed. In neither case can these examples, or any other examples, be compared with the slavery of the blacks. The slave trade, the importation of the enslaved into American colonies, the life of the slave in the West, the antislavery movement and its consequences—shape into a history unlike any other and leave marks that may be ineradicable. Both the history and the marks are recorded in books and pamphlets and ephemera meant to be scanned and tossed away.

It is a history that begins for us with a study of the characteristics of the Negro race by a Dutch physician, Pechlin, who in 1677 developed theories about the color of blacks. Dr. Pechlin decided its cause was a fuliginous humor that filled the tissues. The far more distinguished eighteenth-century French scientist Maupertuis focused his attention, in his *Vénus Physique,* on a white Negro boy, an albino, who prompted innovative thoughts on generation. The second part of Maupertuis' treatise was entitled "Dissertation sur l'Origine des Noirs," a study of Negro racial characteristics especially in African and American blacks.

If interest in blacks had continued to center upon their color, their generation, their physical nature, and their origins, their history and their destiny would have been different indeed. It was not the black as natural phenomenon, but the black as slave whose tragic story has filled bookshelves. It is a story whose pictured reminders are the manacles and irons found in the holds of slave ships.

The first grand-scale grappling with the subject of cruelties of the slave trade took place between May 26, 1789 and March 12, 1790, in Britain's House of Commons. There, with the testimony of merchants and planters, West India agents, creditors of sugar colonies and African residents, the roots of slavery began to be explored. The testimony covered the whole life of the black slave from Africa to the West Indies. It began with the work of slave brokers and witchcraft and the price of slaves; it disclosed details of the voyage: the rubbing of blacks with palm oil, their food and sleep, their illnesses and deaths, the ship masters, the role of irons and fetters. This devastating array of facts was published in a two-part folio volume of *Minutes of the Evidence taken before a Committee of the House of Commons ... relative to the State of the African Slave Trade.* Fortified with charts of ships, their values, and the prices of blacks sold, the work is a prime source for its baleful subject.

Other sources substantiating those *Minutes* followed, emanating mostly from France. During the French Revolution, an *Almanac Historique Nommé Le Messager Boiteux* yielded devastating statistics of the slave trade. Scanning its pages, we learn that during the past few years 104,100 slaves were purchased in Guinea, of whom 80,000 were shipped to the American colonies. The average cost of a slave equaled 100 French ecus. We also learn that the inhuman treatment of slaves frequently led to their suicide.

During the first quarter of the nineteenth century, revealing details of the slave trade were gathered together by advocates of antislavery. One abolitionist committee of the Society of Christian Morality, for example, included in its report—*Faits Relatifs à la Traite des Noirs*—graphic descriptions from documentary evidence of conditions aboard the slave ships bound for the Antilles, Guadeloupe, Martinique, Surinam, San Domingo, and Cuba. The Quakers condemned the slave trade as the homicidal commerce called the "Traite des Noirs."

Neither the slave trade nor the life of the slave in American colonies was concealed from those who pursued the truth of the matter. Those who ran could read, and those who read could read what was called the *Code Noir*. This was a collection of the edicts and legislation regulating commerce and the role of the blacks in the French colonies, Louisiana, and elsewhere. It covered ports and vessels, the sale of slaves, justice and the police, exemptions, merchandise, farm products, conduct of masters. Our copy was of an enlarged edition of 1767. If any citizen doubted that slaves were property bought and sold, a study of the *Code Noir* would set him straight.

A succession of French *arrets* or decrees filled in any missing information. One, dated 1777, concerned the return of blacks, mulattoes and persons of color to the colonies from France. Another, a pivotal decree of September 10, 1786, combined regulations for the export of raw sugar with those for the introduction of black slaves into America.

We did not relish the purchase of pro-slavery writings any more than we relished the purchase of antisemitic writings. We did buy a *Mémoire sur L'Esclavage Des Nègres* by the French colonial commissioner Malouet, who spent a large part of his time in St. Domingo and the adjacent islands during the 1770s. In his *Mémoire* he did suggest that slaves be given better care and education, but, in the present state of affairs, he dismissed any idea of liberating the slaves. They were part of a status quo that might as well continue.

Not merely cupidity but ignorance and ambivalence doubtless played their parts in the attitudes of some anti-blacks. The birth of Jim Crow is surely an instance of this. In 1836, the father of American minstrelsy, Thomas D. Rice, visited London and popularized there what he had already popularized in America—the first famous Negro song and dance. Our London 1837 edition of *The Origin of Jim Crow ... By An American* narrates the career of Jim Crow including his early life on the plantation, his education, his singing and dancing, along with the words of his songs: "The Nigger and the Planter" and "The Original Song of Jump Jim Crow." That Jim Crow was a denigration of the black apparently did not dawn on the father of American minstrelsy or his public.

The only out-and-out consciously conceived eulogy of slavery that crossed our desks was a versified apology for slavery by the Southern planter-poet William J. Grayson, whose *The Hireling and the Slave* was published in 1856 and distributed north of the Mason and Dixon line. In it Grayson wrote that slavery was the "best [system] for the Negro in this country." The circumstance that enabled us to forgive ourselves for harboring *The Hireling and the Slave* on our shelves was our copy's provenance. It bore the bookplate of Augustin Cochin, author of *The Results of Slavery* and *The Results of Emancipation.* Cochin was a noted antislavery writer who doubtless used Grayson's work as a source.

All antislavery writers believed that slavery was morally wrong. Some of them also believed that blacks were the equals of whites. If the egalitarianism of women seemed unconvincing to many, how much more so must have seemed the egalitarianism of the black, especially while he was still enslaved. As we sought books on the former, we welcomed books on the latter. We found in first edition an anonymous French novel published in three volumes in 1789. The tridecker was entitled *Le Nègre comme Il Y A Peu Blancs (The Negro Equaled by Few Whites).* The author—actually Joseph Lavallée—abhorred the *Code Noir,* endorsed the

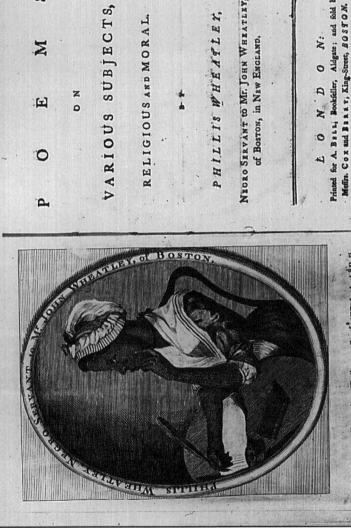

PHILLIS WHEATLEY, NEGRO SERVANT to Mr. JOHN WHEATLEY, of BOSTON.

Published according to Act of Parliament, Sept.r 1. 1773 by Arch.d Bell.
Bookseller N.º 8 near the Saracens Head Aldgate.

P O E M S

ON

VARIOUS SUBJECTS,

RELIGIOUS AND MORAL.

By PHILLIS WHEATLEY,

NEGRO SERVANT to Mr. JOHN WHEATLEY,
of BOSTON, in NEW ENGLAND.

L O N D O N:

Printed for A. BELL, Bookseller, Aldgate; and sold by
Messrs. COX and BERRY, King-Street, BOSTON.

MDCCLXXIII.

Poems by a Former Slave

ability of the blacks, and claimed that they were equaled by few Europeans. Written during a period of revolutionary fervor, the novel was a stepping-stone toward emancipation. In 1801 it would be translated into English and published in Philadelphia accompanied by the poems of the first American black woman poet, Phillis Wheatley.

In due course, Abbé Grégoire joined his championship of the Jews with his significant support of the blacks. His inflammatory *Mémoire* of 1789 endorsed their ability and their rights, exposing abuses in St. Domingo: tabooing of professions and trades, lack of representation in the National Assembly, restrictions of the *Code Noir*. The Abbé's landmark work lauding the intellectual power of the Negro appeared later, in 1808: *De La Littérature Des Nègres, ou Recherches sur leurs facultés intellectuelles*. Besides refuting the prejudiced notion that found blacks inferior to whites morally and intellectually, Grégoire included notices on the life and work of blacks distinguished in science, letters and arts.

In May 1791, the National Convention of France, seeming to recognize the equality of some blacks, had conferred on the mulattoes of St. Domingo all the privileges of French citizens. Not long after, reacting to ensuing reprisals by whites, the decree granting those rights was revoked. Comparison with the British Bill for naturalization of the Jews, repealed the year after it was passed, comes immediately to mind. By August 1791, the St. Domingo plantation slaves and mulattoes began an Insurrection, headed by Toussaint L'Ouverture, details of which are recorded in a succession of pamphlets. By 1793, commissioners sent from France settled the dispute and slavery on the island was abolished. On one island at least, black egalitarianism seemed an acceptable fact.

Etienne-Victor Mentor, a black who had been born in Martinique, became a deputy from St. Domingo to the Council of 500. By the end of the century—in 1798—he pleaded eloquently for the equal ability and the equal treatment of blacks. If they are freemen, let them be treated as freemen. So implored *Etienne Mentor, Représentant du Peuple, Au Directoire Exécutif*.

Along with impassioned demands for egalitarianism toward blacks came printed proofs of the intellectual equality of blacks. One of the most prized of such proofs is *Poems on Various Subjects, Religious and Moral* by Phillis Wheatley, published in London in 1773. Phillis had been sold at auction in Boston in 1761 at age seven, and purchased by John Wheatley, in whose home she was educated. Master Wheatley recognized her ability early on, her linguistic and literary talents, her egalitarianism. At age eighteen, in 1772, she journeyed to England where she was welcomed by the Countess of Huntington. When her poems were published the following year, they were dedicated to the Countess. Among the "Various Subjects" versified by the young poet were "On being brought from Africa" and "To the University of Cambridge, in New-England." Included in the volume were statements of authenticity testified to by the Governor of Massachusetts, Thomas Hutchinson, Samuel Mather, John Hancock, and others. Today these *Poems* by a former slave are prized as a pioneer work in black history. They are more than that, for they are early proof of the intellectual equality of educated blacks and educated whites.

Further proofs were issued from time to time. We had an 1826 volume of *Biographical Sketches and Interesting Anecdotes of Persons of Colour* compiled by Abigail Field Mott. Along with Phillis Wheatley, Mott included Toussaint L'Ouverture and a number of slaves and freedmen from St. Domingo, Jamaica, Barbados and the United States, all of whom supplied the answer to the egalitarian questions: "Am I Not a Man and a Brother?", "Am I Not a Woman and a Sister?"

Both in their deeds and in their writings, the champions of antislavery answered those questions. Many of our antislavery holdings, like many of our prosemitic pleas, were products of the French Revolution. One of them was a fifteen-page pamphlet printed in Paris by the Imprimerie du Patriote François in 1790 and written on behalf of the Société des Amis des Noirs. An attack on the articles of the infamous *Code Noir,* these *Réflexions* offered details of a St. Domingan who had tortured and murdered five of his slaves. On the title-page we found a small vignette of a slave with the recurrent legend: "Ne suis-je pas ton frère?" ("Am I Not Your Brother?")

Pamphlet after pamphlet on French colonialism in the early 1790s gives us the answer. A Creole delegate to the Convention (Philippe-Rose Roume) reports exploitation of slaves in Tobago and demands abolition. An Assembly of Blacks gathers in Paris' Rue Royale and echoes the voice of the crowds; the French statesman Etienne Clavière delivers an address before the National Assembly on behalf of the Society of Friends of the Blacks. An advocate of equal rights, Bonnemain, writing on the *Régéneration des Colonies,* outlines a plan for the gradual emancipation of the slave that will lead to slavery's eradication. His work is illustrated with a folding chart that shows the results of slavery. In a volume entitled *Le Spectateur Français Avant La Révolution* Jacques-Vincent Delacroix includes a discourse on the emancipation of women and a "Lettre d'un Américain sur les Nègres" on freeing the slaves. After the turn of the century French reminders of antislavery appear in published biographies of the great black liberator of St. Domingo, Toussaint L'Ouverture, "Chef des Noirs Insurgés."

From England, meanwhile, other antislavery agitators appear on our bookshelves. One of the greatest was Thomas Clarkson, author of the *Essay on the Slavery and Commerce of the Human Species, Particularly The African.* First written as a Latin dissertation, this was a prize-winner in which the author discussed the life of the plantation slave and also took occasion to mention Phillis Wheatley and her poems. The Bill for total abolition of the slave trade was passed in 1807, and a year later Clarkson published his *History of the Rise, Progress, and Accomplishment of The Abolition of The African Slave-Trade by the British Parliament.* There, one of the two folding plates depicts the inhuman herding of slaves in the ship's hold; a full-page plate shows the slaves' manacles; and a textual woodcut depicts a chained slave kneeling with the familiar legend: "Am I Not a Man and a Brother" which was used as a seal. The slave trade may have been abolished, but slavery still had a way to go. One of the earliest speeches delivered before the House of Commons by William E. Gladstone still advocated gradual emancipation and full compensation to slave owners.

Antislavery in America ran its own course, gathering strength as it gathered advocates. Our earliest literary expression of it was anonymous: *Letters from Virginia,* published in Baltimore in 1816. Amazingly enough, this condemnation of slavery pretended to be a translation from the French. Actually it had been written by George Tucker, who had been born in Bermuda and, at age twelve, sent to Virginia where he later practiced law and taught at Jefferson's University. Besides attacking slavery, his *Letters* ridiculed the planters who sustained it.

It was an American black—Prince Sanders—who compiled our *Haytian Papers* in 1818. These official documents of Haiti included not only extracts from registers and proclamations, but reflections on the abolition of the slave trade.

Step by slow step, book by book, pamphlet by pamphlet, a nation half slave and half free was being led toward emancipation during the first half of the nineteenth century. In 1837, Elijah Lovejoy was murdered in Alton, Illinois, for defending his abolitionist press. In May of the same year, a National Woman's Anti-Slavery Convention was held in New York at which Angelina Grimké was appointed to present an appeal for the slaves to the people of the free states. Another outcome of that Convention was an antislavery token that to us represented an historic moment and a union of two causes: feminism and antislavery. On its recto were the words: "Am I Not A Woman & A Sister" surrounding a kneeling female slave with right arm uplifted and the date 1838. On the verso appeared the words: "United States of America" surrounding a laurel wreath, the word "Liberty" and the date 1838.

Alexis de Tocqueville was the author not only of *Democracy in America,* but of a *Rapport ... relative aux Esclaves des colonies.* As a member of an official commission inquiring into the situation of slavery in the French colonies, especially the West Indies, the distinguished author, recommending gradual emancipation, proclaimed that slavery could not endure.

At the same time, in 1839, one of the greatest of our abolitionists, Theodore Dwight Weld, helped ensure that slavery *would* not endure. Weld's *American Slavery As It Is* was subtitled *Testimony of A Thousand Witnesses* when it was published in New York by the American Anti-Slavery Society. It contained testimony from newspapers published in the slave states detailing the atrocities, punishments, cruelties, tortures and privations inflicted upon slaves. It also contained the personal narratives of the Grimké sisters regarding the barbarous treatment of women slaves. Weld's book would provide a chief source for the little woman who, with *Uncle Tom's Cabin,* would help make a great war.

Intermittently, we acquired a few of the stepping stones to that war. On August 1, 1844, on the tenth anniversary of the emancipation of slaves in the West Indies, Ralph Waldo Emerson delivered his celebratory *Address ... in The Court-House in Concord, Massachusetts.* He described the event as "singular in the history of civilization," an event by which "a man is added to the human family."

The failure of the United States to emancipate all its slaves was highlighted in 1850 with the biography of one of the country's most famous slaves. Sojourner Truth had been a northern slave before her emancipation in 1828 by the State of New York. The *Narrative* of her life by Olive Gilbert provided graphic details of Sojourner's auction and masters, her escape, the sale of her son, the brutalities she suffered. Moreover, it included certificates to her character by William Lloyd Garrison and other distinguished abolitionists, along with an article on slavery by Theodore Weld.

Former slaves were not only subjects of biographies but writers of autobiographies. Two years after *Uncle Tom's Cabin,* the fugitive slave James Watkins wrote the *Narrative* of his own life. Born on a Maryland plantation, he escaped to Britain, and his book described his escape route along with his comments on the Fugitive Slave Law.

The antislavery writings that we accumulated did not include the great landmarks. We never had *Uncle Tom's Cabin* in first edition, for example. What we did acquire were bits and pieces that showed the way the winds were blowing, that threw a glimmer of light upon the national attitude toward slavery, that led on to a divided nation and a great war. Our holdings on black history ended with a trifle, but a telling trifle. Its full title was *The New House that Jack Built. An Original American Version.* It was published in New York in 1865 as our great and terrible Civil War was ending. And it sold for a dime, for it was a Beadle Dime Book. In it Jack, the laborer, builds the Union with the building materials of civil rights, free speech and free worship. Secession is pictured as a dog; slavery as a rat. Here was an illustrated dime book in original printed wrappers that castigated slavery and exalted the Union. Here was indeed *multum in parvo*—the beginning of a national retribution that would never be sufficient however long it might endure.

X

The Lure of Firsts

To be first is generally thought to be foremost. We seek firsts in every phase of life. Who was the first to conquer a mountain or open up a profession? Who was the first to discover a country or explore a land? Who was the first to paint a special portrait or build a particular dwelling? And with the "Who" goes the "What." What was the first textbook published in a certain country—the first play performed—the first illustration by a great painter—the first appearance of this, the first description of that?

It lures the mind, this pursuit of *firstness*. Although the word *firstness* does not appear in dictionaries, surely it is more apt than the erudite *primacy*. To pursue firstness is to pursue the beginning, and the beginning of anything is always a pot of gold for the eager researcher.

To chase after beginnings, after firstness, is never more intriguing than when it is conducted in the printed pages of early books. To prove priority is usually difficult and sometimes impossible, but in the course of our decades in antiquarian books, we think we have stumbled upon firsts from time to time. Though they may not have been earth-shaking, they provided their share of excitement.

We had, for example, an historical tragedy by Pierre de Belloy, *Le Siège de Calais (The Siege of Calais)* produced in 1765. Dramatizing the French surrender to Edward III of England in 1347, the play was filled with overtones of eighteenth-century French regret and patriotism. Unfortunately, in this instance, we had the tragedy in first edition. It was, we learned, another later edition that would have been our pot of gold. *The Siege of Calais,* we discovered, would become the first play published in what was called "French America," where it was seen through the press by the Comte d'Estaing, a French admiral who had fought with Lafayette in the American Revolution. The Count moved on to Martinique and other islands in the French West Indies, where his enthusiasm for Belloy's play induced him to have it published. As for us, we had learned something. Besides, we did have the first edition of what had not yet become a "first."

A true dramatic first that we did have was the first attempt to place William Shakespeare on the French stage. Jean François Ducis' adaptation of *Hamlet,* "Imitée de L'Anglois," was first performed by the Comédie Française on September 30, 1769. The Paris 1770 edition joined *The Siege of Calais* on the shelves we devoted to the theater.

It was not a playwright but a performer whose first concert in America was immortalized in our *Programme of Mademoiselle Jenny Lind's Concert. With the Words of the Airs in Italian, German, Swedish & English.* The famous Swedish singer first enchanted her audience in September 1850 at New York's Castle Garden. Our program of the memorable theatrical and operatic event included short biographical sketches of Jenny, her impresario P.T. Barnum, and the baritone. It also included selections from Rossini and Bellini, Weber and Mendelssohn, as well as a "Greeting to America" with words by Bayard Taylor. Besides a view of the interior of Castle Garden with Jenny on stage, the program offered advertisements from Tiffany, Brady's Portrait Gallery, and Genin the Hatter who had paid $225 for the first ticket sold at auction.

Our Jenny Lind program also provided us with a list of the members of the orchestra. All lists are important to antiquarians whether they are lists of people or of books. The first such lists have a continuing appeal. Such lists of books we term in deference bibliographies, and when they are the first to be compiled they take on added significance. We were fortunate to acquire *A Catalogue of Chymicall Books* compiled by William Cooper, the seventeenth-century bookseller-auctioneer of "the Pelican in Little Britain, London," for it is the first English bibliography of chemical and alchemical writings. Listing between five- and six-hundred works, it also includes writings on husbandry and mineralogy. We had this first in its first separate edition of 1675.

Another first listing that lured us was the *Catalogue Raisonné* of works by Rembrandt compiled by a French antiquarian, Gersaint. This earliest attempt to catalogue the great artist's engravings listed his heads, portraits and landscapes, along with his doubtful works and the works of his pupils.

It was no list of engravings but a portrait that we found in a Luther sermon of 1519, purchased, incidentally, during our first buying trip abroad, that proved one of our most exciting firsts. We have mentioned the find briefly elsewhere, but as the first printed work to contain a portrait of the Reformer Martin Luther, the *Sermon geprediget tzu Leipsgk* deserves more than a mere mention. The medallion portrait on the title-page shows Martin Luther in his monk's habit and biretta. He is pictured within a circular roll intersected by a rose bearing the words: "Doctor. Martinvs. Lvtter. Avgvstiner: Wittenb." Both the portrait and the roll are within a heavy black frame. The likeness of the Reformer precedes the well-known Cranach portrait executed in 1520, and, although previously unknown, it is now recognized as the earliest portrait of Luther. This remarkable first we acquired in first edition, first issue.

The great artists remembered today for their paintings in the museums of the world sometimes began their careers as illustrators of books, and so planted firsts on printed pages rather than on canvas. When, in 1608, Philip Rubens published a study on various aspects of Roman life, his brother obliged by designing five illustrations of Roman charioteers, togas and ornaments. The author of the book had studied in Italy and served as librarian-secretary to Cardinal Ascanio Colonna. When he returned to Antwerp his treatise on Rome was published by the great House of Plantin-Moretus. The illustrations, engraved by Cornelis Galle, had been drawn by Philip's brother. And so, the *Electorvm Libri II* of 1608 became a first of high interest. Philip's brother happened to be none other than Peter-Paul Rubens. The *Electorvm Libri II* was the first book illustrated by the most distinguished of Flemish painters.

For everything there is a beginning. It needs only to be searched out. Our firsts in art history were joined by an interesting and unusual architectural first. This was an elephant folio of 1776 adorned with twenty full-page plates prepared by a Parisian architect, d'Albaret. According to him, after the conquest of the West Indies, Europeans who settled there disregarded the area's peculiar climate and continued their native customs in architectural matters. As a result, they suffered severely the effects of storms and earthquakes, tropical rains and intense heat. Monsieur d'Albaret proceeded to introduce his innovative functional architecture adapted to the West Indies. Here were plans and elevations for rooms and piazzas, doors and balustrades, walls and cornices—all designed to offset earthquake and torrential rain. The *Différens Projets Relatifs Au Climat Et A La Manière La Plus Convenable De Bâtir Dans Les Pays Chauds, Et Plus Particulièrement Dans Les Indes Occidentales* was a long title for this first in functional architecture for the heat of the West Indies.

The West Indies and especially the United States have yielded fascinating firsts to us. One of them was the first atlas of America. The work of Cornelius Wytfliet, it described "a part of the globe entirely unknown to the ancients," recounted the voyages of Columbus, Pizarro and Cortes, and included maps of Cuba, the "peninsula" of California, Virginia, Florida, New France, New Spain. Our edition of 1611, though not the first, conveyed the newness of the New World to us.

We were a very new United States of America in 1778 when our *Recueil des Loix Constitutives des Colonies Angloises, Confédérées sous la dénomination D'Etats-Unis de L'Amérique-Septentrionale* was published. The first such collection, it included the Declaration of Independence, the Articles of Confederation, Congressional Acts, and the State Constitutions. Its dedicatory epistle, addressed to Benjamin Franklin, declared the law a monument to democracy. In our hierarchy of American firsts, this "monument" was surpassed by our first French edition of the *Constitutions* of the thirteen original states. It was at Franklin's suggestion that La Rochefoucauld translated the work, and, enriched with over fifty footnotes by Franklin, the *Constitutions des Treize Etats-Unis de L'Amérique* appeared in 1783 in an edition of only 600 copies. This was indeed a landmark work. It was also a first, for on its title-page was printed for the first time in any book the seal of the United States: the eagle, the stars, the stripes.

Franco-American relations were close in those early days of the republic. A pioneer text published in 1792 brought them closer and strengthened the ties between the two countries. *L'Abeille Françoise* was the first French textbook of its kind published in the United States. An anthology of the writings of Rousseau and Fénelon, Voltaire and Montesquieu, Bernardin de Saint-Pierre and others, it helped introduce French thought into the country. It had been compiled by Joseph Nancrede, tutor of French at Harvard who later became a productive Franco-American bookseller-publisher. Subscribers to the volume included John Quincy Adams and John Hancock, Josiah Quincy and the printer Isaiah Thomas.

Another of our American firsts is also a Franco-American production. The *Mémoires de Paul Jones,* published in Paris in 1798, is the first life of the celebrated naval officer in the American Revolution, John Paul Jones, the popular hero credited with the memorable statement: "I have just begun to fight." The memoir was not intended for general publication; Jones wished only five copies made. He is said to have presented the manuscript to Louis XVI; the translation was made by the French journalist Jean-François André. Published in 1798 the volume, with profile portrait of Jones and, below, the engagement of *Bonhomme Richard* and *Serapis,* is the earliest source for a memorable American life.

Even when part of a book is derivative, a *first* may be lurking in its pages. The French voyager André Thevet's great work on *Les singvlaritez de la France Antarctique, autrement nommée Amérique,* containing one of the earliest accounts of Canada, for example, also contains the first description of a quadruped that played an unparalleled role in American history—the buffalo.

As thousands of Americans were sustained by food and warmth from the buffalo, the Israelites, wandering in the wilderness, found sustenance from manna. The manna, it was believed, was from heaven, miraculously supplied. Not so, according to the first book on the subject. An Italian physician, Altomari, in his *De mannae differentijs ... ratione* of 1562, gave us the first treatise to prove where manna came from. It was, according to the author, an exudate of a tree, the flowering ash, and its nourishment was less spiritual than physical.

Most, but not all of our conceptual *firsts* were found by us in first edition. A few we had in later editions or in translations. In the case of non-conceptual *firsts,* however—books whose *firstness* derives not from their content but from their publishing history—it is necessary to search out first editions with knowledge and determination. Much has been written about the pursuit of first editions, especially of great works of the past, and even more especially of twentieth-century modern firsts. We refrain from treading on those crowded paths. Instead, we recall one or two first editions from each of four different centuries whose stories seem to us worth telling.

Our first treasured example is the first edition in pocket format of Dante's *Le Terze Rime.* A manuscript of Dante's masterpiece was submitted by the Italian humanist Cardinal Bembo to the greatest publisher of all time—Aldus Manutius of Venice. The result appeared in 1502, the *Divine Comedy* in pocket format, a poem written in the early fourteenth century, now a landmark of the Aldine Press. At its end was the Aldine Anchor. Our copy was bound in gilt olive morocco with handsome interlaced double gilt lines and fleurons by Bedford, a book that breathes the spirit of the Renaissance but a book for every age, for all time.

The divine Michelangelo—painter, architect, sculptor—was also poet. His verses for the most part concerned ideal and Platonic love and were addressed to Tommaso de' Cavalieri and to the artist's friend Vittoria Colonna, herself a fine poet. His poems remained in manuscript during his life. Michelangelo died in 1564. It was not until nearly sixty years later that the *Rime* of Michelangelo Buonarroti saw print. The poems were collected by his nephew, Michelangelo Buonarroti the Younger, and published in Florence by the Giunta Press in 1623. The first edition of the divine Michelangelo's poems was a seventeenth-century affair.

Had there been best-seller lists in early seventeenth-century Spain, Cervantes' *Don Quixote* would have leaped to the number one spot. Yet it was not till half a century later—in 1652—that the first complete English edition—our edition—of his masterpiece was published. It had been translated earlier on by Thomas Shelton, who did the work at the request "of a very deere friend that was desirous to understand the subject." The translation was robust, reproducing the spirit and broad humanity of the original. *The History of The Valorous and VVitty-Knight-Errant, Don Quixote, Of the Mancha,* issued in London, contained two parts. Now all of England could ridicule romances of chivalry and follow the adventures of Don Quixote and Sancho Panza. This first English edition with the two parts together became an important first for us.

Another delayed seventeenth-century first edition was Sir Walter Raleigh's *The Cabinet-Council.* Its sub-title explains the matter: "Containing the Cheif Arts of Empire, And Mysteries of State ... Published By John Milton." The manuscript of Raleigh's study on government had been entrusted to Milton by a learned man. After he had held on to it many years, Milton added a brief preface and had the work published in London in 1658. Thus the great seventeenth-century English poet helped create the first edition of Raleigh's *Cabinet-Council.* Our copy bore a dated bookplate recalling an earlier association between Raleigh and the Essex family: that of Algernon Capell, Earl of Essex, 1701.

Our eighteenth-century first made its appearance and its impact very early in the century. Sir Isaac Newton's *Opticks* was first published in London in 1704. A landmark in the history of science, it covered the author's experiments on the spectrum, his conclusions on color and light, his explanation of the rainbow, his thoughts on the polarization of light. This first edition was joined on our shelves by the first Latin edition, *Optice: ... Libri Tres* issued in 1706. The Latin edition had its own claim to fame, since it was the first edition to offer Newton's views on the double refraction of Iceland spar, and since it included six more queries than the first English edition.

The eighteenth century gave us an excellent example of still another delayed first edition. The autobiography of the distinguished Italian goldsmith Benvenuto Cellini remained in manuscript long after his death, far longer than the poems of his compatriot Michelangelo. Cellini died in 1571; his *Vita* was not published until 1728 when it was issued in Naples from the original manuscript, but with a false and undated Cologne imprint. To compound the problem, this first genuine edition was followed sixty-four years later by a counterfeit edition. The counterfeit naturally bore the same imprint as the true first edition: "Cologne: Martel," without date. Actually it was published in Florence by the firm of Bartolini in 1792. The two editions are distinguishable, one from the other, by one or two technicalities including the number of lines in the dedication leaf. Both editions present the text of one of the most important of Renaissance memoirs, reflecting Cellini's accomplishments and the spirit of his age. The genuine edition, however, is the first—not the counterfeit. Nonetheless, both editions sit comfortably together on a bookshelf.

Our nineteenth-century first is, like our Cervantes, the first English edition of a classic. In it the "Father of Scientific Socialism" analyzed the economic structure of society and applied the materialist concept of history and the labor theory of value. The first volume of Karl Marx's *Das Kapital* was published in 1867, to be followed by two additional volumes after his death. Our English translation was the work of Samuel Moore and Marx's son-in-law Edward Aveling, and it included the revisions of Engels. It appeared in London in two volumes in 1887, a first that made available and intelligible to English readers the concepts of a Marxist economy.

If first English editions of foreign works are sometimes almost as desirable as original first editions, first American editions of European writings have—at least to us as Americans—an even more seductive appeal. They show us the way political and literary winds from abroad were blowing; they tell us which foreign influences were paramount; they tell us not only what was being read here, but what was being thought. And indeed, one of our favorite first American editions was that of Karl Marx's *Capital,* a good companion for our first English edition. Published by Appleton of New York in 1889, it introduced American readers to a revolutionary view of labor and capital to which they would react for years to come.

Much of cultural Europe came to America by way of books. We tracked down what we believe may be the first appearance here of lines from Shakespeare's *Othello* in the first American edition of Burton's *Lectures on Female Education and Manners* published in New York in 1794. The text—a study of women's education and recommended reading—appealed to the new republic. Even more interesting, we found at the head of the lecture on evil-speaking, Iago's famous lines on "Good name in man or woman." The first collected Shakespeare did not appear here till 1795/96 and the first separate edition of *Othello* till 1807. It is quite possible that *Othello* was first quoted here in our Burton *Lectures on Female Education.*

British medicine came to America almost hand in hand with William Shakespeare. In 1795 the Albany publisher Spencer issued the first American edition of Matthew Baillie's *Morbid Anatomy of Some of the Most Important Parts of the Human Body.* The volume had many firsts attached to it: it was the first book in English devoted to the subject; it contained the first definition of *cirrhosis;* and in first American edition it doubtless enabled citizens of the United States to relieve their ills with home remedies.

A year later the political opinions of the young republic were swayed by a first American edition. William Godwin's *Enquiry concerning Political Justice* was issued in Philadelphia in two volumes in 1796. Godwin's landmark book discussing man in society, government, the social contract, revolution and tyrannicide, crime and punishment, property, legislative and executive power, gave food for thought to a people shaping themselves into a nation. Our copy was particularly interesting, reflecting as it did the adverse opinion of an early owner who signed himself "W.L." In Volume I, W.L. wrote a warning critique: "Reader this Book contains the most subtil Deistical poison of any in the English Language."

One by one the greats of England and Europe made their appearance in this country. In 1802 Isaiah Thomas, Jr., of Worcester, Massachusetts, brought out the first American edition of Montesquieu's classic *The Spirit of Laws.* This first study of comparative political theory analyzed the interrelations of commerce and climate and laid the foundations of geographical determinism. In later editions it would influence succeeding generations of Americans. In first American edition it reaffirmed our founding fathers.

Americans, whose future depended so heavily on European immigration and settlement, could study the phenomenon of population in 1809 when the publisher Milligan of Georgetown, D.C. circulated Malthus' famous *Essay on the Principle of Population.* In that great work they could study too the perils of over-population and the checks to population in "underdeveloped" peoples like the American Indians.

It was not until 1818 that Samuel Johnson's *Dictionary of The English Language* achieved American edition. Webster's *Compendious Dictionary* preceded it in 1806 and Webster's *American Dictionary* followed it in 1828. The Johnson lexicon was published in Philadelphia by Moses Thomas who later became an auctioneer, and it included a history of the language, an English grammar, and Walker's Principles of English Pronunciation. A two-volume set in large thick quarto format, adorned with a frontispiece portrait of Samuel Johnson, it helped put words into the mouths of young America.

One of the fascinations of early books is the fact that nothing about them is ever cut-and-dried. Book lore is no mathematical science. Books sometimes resemble living creatures, changeable in reputation, dependent upon shifts in popular taste. For this reason the lure of firsts, that gave us the title of this chapter, is sometimes not the lure of firsts, but the lure of later editions, of editions reprinted to meet the demands of a specific audience or to warn of or rejoice in a revolutionary event. Such reprints may be far more meaningful than their first editions, for they not only carry their original message but reflect the needs and demands of a later time.

We have written elsewhere about two of the most obvious examples of such reprints.* One is William Wollaston's *The Religion of Nature Delineated,* a philosophical work of no great interest in first edition. Its third edition, however, was set in type by a young compositor working in Palmer's printing house in London who later wrote a refutation of the work. The name of that printer-philosopher was Benjamin Franklin. Similarly, the first edition of Leopold Mozart's study of violin playing,

---

* See Leona Rostenberg and Madeleine B. Stern, *Old & Rare: Forty Years in the Book Business* (Santa Monica 1988) p. 173.

though most valuable, is a straightforward manual on the subject; in second edition, however, something new was added: a prefatory note regarding a delay in publication occasioned by the musical tour of the author's virtuoso children. Since one of Leopold Mozart's virtuoso children was Wolfgang Amadeus, and since this is the first reference to him in any book, the second edition of the *Gründliche Violinschule* is to us far more desirable than the first.

There are surely hundreds of significant reprints that may yield more excitement than their first appearances. A few of them have passed through our hands and given us stories to tell.

The first illustrated edition of Vasari's great biographical anthology, *The Lives of the Painters,* was published in 1568. There is no denying its importance, its beauty, and its value. But still rarer is a separate edition of one of those *Lives* taken from the *Vite* and published the same year of 1568. That separate is devoted to the life of Michelangelo. Published with a specially printed title-page, a dedicatory leaf and a leaf of register and colophon, this *Vita Del Gran Michelagnolo Bvonarroti*—basically a reprint—is truly a rarity in the literature of art.

Most of our treasured reprints were outcomes of the French Revolution. In breaking with the past, the French Revolution reached out to the past, often to the English past which was made to serve the French present. The fate of the Stuart monarch Charles I, tried and executed in 1649, suggested much that was pertinent to the French readership of 1792. The Paris publisher Lepetit grasped the opportunity to reprint the *Rélation Véritable De La Mort Cruelle Et Barbare De Charles I, Roi D'Angleterre,* containing documentary evidence regarding the monarch's tyrannicide. With its preliminary Notice to the Reader on the death of kings, the volume pointed an unmistakable moral in 1792. The parallel to French Revolutionary affairs was tacit, but it was there.

In the same way John Milton's *Defense of the English People,* justifying the action of the regicides of Charles I, provided fuel for the Revolutionary flame. A reprint of the *Defensio,* published in Paris in 1789, was seized and destined for burning. Mirabeau, who is said to have rescued it from the fire, proceeded to abridge it, translate it into French, and publish it, first as the *Doctrine de Milton sur la royauté,* and as *Théorie de la royauté, d'après la doctrine de Milton,* and finally in 1792 as the *Défense Du Peuple Anglais.* Here was another reminder to Louis XVI and his supporters of the fate of an earlier despot. According to the title-page, this was a book that could clarify current conditions in France. A fascinating reprint, it links two cataclysmic ages, as well as two great names.

In reprints the citizen of Geneva exerted strong influence during the French Revolution. The republican ideology of Rousseau's *Contrat Social*, first issued in 1762, appealed to Revolutionary theorists, and at least fifteen reprints of the work that based all government upon the consent of the governed were published between 1790 and 1795. Time and again readers were reminded that the sovereignty of the people lies in the general will of the people, that the state is an organism endowed with a communal conscience. Through reprints Rousseau reached and influenced French Revolutionaries. Indeed one reprint of the *Contrat Social* published by Didot in 1792 appeared as a 32mo, a pocket edition strongly resembling a breviary—which, apparently, it was for the French Revolution.

Sometimes a reprint gains its importance from something added or altered. We think of Baudelaire's Poe in French translation. The author of *Les Fleurs du Mal* regarded Poe as his alter ego and, according to some critics, his translation of *The Narrative of Arthur Gordon Pym*, published in Paris in 1858, is better than the original. In 1889, Mallarmé translated Poe's poems into French prose, and to that edition were added illustrations by the great French impressionist Edouard Manet. Such reprints not only vie with first editions but occasionally surpass them.

First editions continue to lure. In them we can find the earliest embodiments of literary masterpieces or political manifestoes, innovations in art or scientific discoveries. We hold them in our hands and find ourselves witnesses of newness, from a medical panacea to the shaping of a nation. Later editions may yield their secrets reluctantly, but they too often open doors. We have but to enter to find ourselves at the beginning of things.

XI

The Press: Exotic and Uncommon

Anything exotic or unusual appears infrequently and is uncommon. Exotic or unusual issues of the printing press have come to us at long, long intervals and have never crowded our shelves. When they do appear, they are unmistakable. They reveal almost in a flash, from a peculiar typography or a remarkable imprint, a title or a printer's name, that here is something quite out of the ordinary, something—as Webster defines *exotic*—"excitingly strange." The few examples we have had certainly excited us. This chapter, therefore, should be both very short and very striking.

In the mid-nineteenth century, the Royal Printing House of Vienna published a type specimen book that listed and illustrated many of the so-called exotic types. Among them were types Aethiopic and Albanian, Greek and Hebrew, Arabic and Aramaic, Chaldaic and Chinese, Korean, Cyrillic, Etruscan, Illyric, Japanese and Celtic. Such types sound strange to modern American ears, but they also entice, just as visits to exotic countries entice the anticipating traveler. Early printing houses tried them from time to time, usually for a well defined purpose.

The great sixteenth-century houses—the Aldine, the Estienne— were of course equipped with exotic type faces. Robert Estienne was appointed royal printer for Hebrew and Latin in 1539, and, along with the faculty of the Collège de France, encouraged studies in ancient tongues. The Hebrew and Greek *Alphabets* he issued in the same year of 1539 include keys to pronunciation as well as numerals and the Decalogue.

It is more surprising to find that Hebrew letter was used at the press of the Collège des Lombards in Paris for another 1539 printing of the *Alphabetum Hebraicum*. This extremely rare printing has a commentary by the professor of Hebrew at the Collège de France, Agathius Guidacerius, who had fled to France after the Sack of Rome in 1527.

Interest in Hebrew scholarship evinced itself early in the sixteenth century, and the availability of Hebrew type is therefore not surprising. In a later printing establishment, however, not only Hebrew and Greek letters were in use, but an extraordinary array of exotic types. At the polyglot printing house founded by the Vatican in the seventeenth century could be found 44 fonts cut by the masters of the press, among them the following amazing assortment: Etruscan, Iberian, Chaldean, Arabic, Brahmin, Hindustani, Indian, Tibetan, Persian, Ethiopic, Armenian, Slavonic, Cyrillic, Coptic, Burmese. Early in the seventeenth century the Vatican created the Congregatio Propagandae Fidei, and to implement its purpose established a printing house. The Congregation for the Propaganda of the Faith did just what its name announced: it communicated the Catholic faith to the newly discovered or remote lands of the world. Its printing press was its right arm, providing alphabets and Biblical excerpts to propagate the faith among the heathen,

The first *Alphabet* issued by the press was the *Alphabetvm Ibericvm, sive Georgianvm* (the *Iberic or Georgian Alphabet)* in 1629. Most of the Congregatio's alphabets offered the Lord's Prayer in native letters, and many also included the Ten Commandments, the Ave Maria, and the Apostles' Creed. Their title-pages bore the seal of the Congregation, and some alphabets also offered one or more folding plates. During the eighteenth century the press was directed by the philological scholar Amaduzzi who brought it to its apogee. Amaduzzi also compiled a bibliography of its exotic alphabets. We have had a few collections of them from time to time, but never of course all of them. Individually or in collection, they embody the purpose and power of the Vatican. Here in these alphabets Rome strove to convert the infidel and draw an exotic world into its fold.

For political rather than religious purposes, seventeenth- and eighteenth-century France also found the press an irresistible ally. Many of its printer-publishers avoided the beaten path. During the mid-seventeenth century, when civil wars—the Frondes—were raging in France, and Cardinal Mazarin dominated the political scene, thousands of so-called Mazarinades were published—pamphlets intended to sway their readers to left or to right. One, issued in 1649, was written by the printer-booksellers of Paris—*Remerciment Des Imprimevrs A Monseignevr Le Cardinal Mazarin (Thanks of the Printers to Cardinal Mazarin)*. The printers thank the Cardinal for the current warfare because it has increased their business! "Publishing," they declare, "has become the happiest profession of Paris—not a day passes that the Parisian presses do not issue more than a volume of pamphlets which weigh down the apprentices and delivery boys."

At no time was this statement truer than during the French Revolution when "Imprimeries" sprang up under individual direction or were attached to every department of government to express an independent political philosophy. One of the most interesting of the Revolutionary "Imprimeries" was that of the Cercle Social founded in 1789 by the French publicist and writer Bonneville. It was located on Paris' Rue du Théatre Français where Bonneville lived and the members of the Cercle Social met. It offered books from stock authored by Rousseau and Voltaire, Mirabeau and Condorcet, and it announced new works and works in the press including journals and pamphlets. The press of the Cercle Social was one of numerous presses established in Revolutionary France to convert a political infidel to the printer's way of thinking. Through the medium of the press the printer's message was voiced.

A violent tract on the proceedings of the French Revolutionary National Assembly was printed in 1790. Though its contents were fiery, its title was non-commital: *Aristarque A Zoile*. What was interesting about the pamphlet was its imprint: "Imprimé sous la Direction de M. Clousier, Imprimeur du Roi, par les Enfans-Aveugles." ("Printed under the Direction of M. Clousier, King's Printer, by the Blind Children."). In this particular instance the imprint may have been of a satirical nature, but in later instances, especially in the nineteenth century, the blind did work as printers and an embossed alphabet for the blind was created—a different exotic type designed to sustain rather than to convert.

The Institution for the Blind in Paris, founded in 1784, was subsequently directed by Dr. Sébastien Guillie. Guillie, a master of educational techniques for the sightless, was also a close observer of their emotional and psychological condition. His *Essai Sur L'Instruction des Aveugles* was among the early books on the subject, covering not only instruction and occupations for the blind but the lives of famous blind persons. Printed in 1817 at the Institution he directed, it included an engraved frontispiece, a chart, and 21 delicately engraved plates showing the blind at work, weaving, knitting, spinning, playing musical instruments, writing, and— of particular interest—setting type and printing. The book itself, richly and beautifully illustrated, was "Imprimé par les Aveugles," a fact that raises it to high significance not only in the history of the blind but in the history of unusual printing.

The history and work of the Institution for the Blind were recorded around 1825 in a *Notice Historique*. In it the place was described: its kitchen, refectory, and chapel, its school administration, faculty and lessons. The work of the blind was stressed, particularly such as related to the book arts. The Institution's printing presses and method used were explained along with book binding techniques. The *Notice* itself bore the uncommon and heartening imprint: "Imprimé par les Aveugles."

The first practical type for the blind was invented by William Moon, author of *Light For The Blind* first published in London in 1873. In that volume Moon described and explained his embossed type which was easily read by the tactile method, and went on to discuss its introduction into England and elsewhere. The two plates included a specimen of Moon's type for the blind in various languages and his embossed alphabet for the blind.

The study of uncommon printing types and presses sometimes turns up an uncommon printer. A prime and universally known example would be Benjamin Franklin whose work in printing was eclipsed by his other accomplishments. We came across four notable men whose double lives included a life as printer. Each came from a different century. All were French. Two had violent ends.

Etienne Dolet* was without doubt the finest printer of this quartet. His Lyons establishment produced a small collection of great rarities issued between 1538 and 1546. Elegantly executed, handsomely printed, his translation of Cicero's letters, his work on Francis I of France, his poems to Rabelais and Marot exhibited his superb presswork. Other Dolet writings revealed not only his scholarship and humanism but his dangerous freethinking. Charged with blasphemy, atheism and sedition, Etienne Dolet was branded a heretic and burned in 1546 in the Place Maubert.

Nicolas Catherinot of Bourges was a seventeenth-century local historian who took detailed notes on the conditions and events of his neighboring provinces. From his notes he compiled what he called "libri brevi," a series of antiquarian news sheets that reanimated the annals of Bourges and Berry with information not to be found elsewhere. Catherinot not only wrote those pamphlets but published and sold them. To find one of these exciting ephemera issued in quarto format between 1650 and 1683 is gratifying. To find a collection of them is an antiquarian's sheer delight. Once, many years ago, we found 23 of them bound together. More recently we found a collection of 44. Catherinot may be

---

*For a more detailed account, see Rostenberg and Stern, *Old & Rare: Forty Years in the Book Business* (Santa Monica 1988) p. 208.

recalled by scholars today more as a provincial historian than as a printer. But had he not been a printer-bookseller, his work as provincial historian would probably not have survived at all.

Far better known is our uncommon printer of the eighteenth century. The Paris imprint, "Imprimerie de Marat," alerts us to the fact that
the great French Revolutionary, Jean-Paul Marat, had a printing establishment and during and in between his political activities worked as
printer. We have had several of the pamphlets that rolled from his press.
Perhaps the most exciting was his *Discours ... Sur la défense de Louis XVI*
in which he expressed his opinion that the king must die to expiate his
crimes. As a matter of fact, both the king and Marat, "Ami du Peuple,"
would perish the same year, the former guillotined, the latter assassinated by Charlotte Corday.

Both Catherinot and Marat were primarily printers of their own
writings. A greater and far better-known writer printed the work of others. Honoré de Balzac, author of the *Contes Drolatiques, Eugénie Grandet,
Père Goriot*—of some 85 novels in 20 years—set up a printing establishment on Paris' Rue des Marais in 1825. Of the numerous volumes that
emerged from his press, we have had three. Dupin's *La Liberté
Individuelle* of 1826 was a plea for individual liberty and a diatribe against
arbitrary arrest. Cadet's *Observations sur l'expédition de 1827 pour le Pole
Nord* was a pamphlet on an 1827 expedition to the North Pole. Pierre
Victor Besenval's *Mémoires* recorded in two volumes the life of a Swiss
general in the service of France. All were fine examples of Balzac's presswork, and of the role of a great novelist in the printing trade.

The output of exotic presses, of uncommon printing establishments, must be seen to be appreciated; it is sometimes as exotic and
uncommon as they are. Early in our business career, during our second
journey abroad in search of books, we found a treatise on a Celtic people
of Upper Italy who founded the city of Milan. Written and printed in
1541 by Bonaventura Castiglione, an Italian antiquarian, it elucidated an
early phase of Italian history. But that was not the reason we acquired it.
In reality the quarto volume was an experiment in type design.
Castiglione used, apparently to draw attention to and animate his theme,
an unusually upright italic designed with swash letters of great appeal.
The result was the production of curious and beautiful italic characters
that we found not only attractive but most uncommon.

Diamonds for the Medicis

Today we are familiar with modern verses classified as concrete poetry because of their typographical appearance. To find a foreshadowing of this in the sixteenth century is arresting. We did so with our Paris 1543 edition of Theocritus' bucolic idyls in Greek. The typographical arrangement of some of the verses formed a concrete design far in advance of the technique used for George Herbert's verses in the seventeenth century and for the concrete poetry of modern times.

One of the most striking typographical designs we have found illustrating—dramatizing—the subject of a book appears in Pierre Boissat's *Le Brillant de la Royne* published in Lyons in 1613. This detailed biographical study of the Medici family was written especially to honor the French queen-mother Marie de Medici. The brilliant glory of the Medicis is brilliantly and immediately depicted in the superbly engraved title-page. There the eye is caught by a large diamond pendant suspended from a fleur-de-lis representing members of the Medici family, representing indeed the text and tenor of the entire book. Here in a single typographic design are the glitter and lustre of the Medici.

Many devotional books lend themselves to unusual typographical treatment. Pierre Moreau, a seventeenth-century Parisian writing master, manufactured punches and matrices in calligraphic style to adorn two works by Jean Baudoin: *Les Sainctes Prières* and *Les Saintes Métamorphoses,* both published by Moreau in Paris in 1644. Each page of text is printed within a delicate border of scrolls, vases, putti, arabesques, giving the illusion of delicate penmanship and resulting in what might be called a "trick book"—a "trick book" in the service of the Lord, an exotic offering on an altar.

At the opposite end of the spectrum, but also in the mid-seventeenth century, *The Bloody Court; or, The Fatall Tribunall* was published in London. An anti-Cromwellian explosion, this anonymous pamphlet was issued secretly "by a rural pen" to describe the "Bloody Conspiracies," "The Boody Tragedy of all Tragedies against King, Lords and Commons," and the trial of Charles I. The "bloody" reign of Cromwell is not the only sanguinary element of this work. *The Bloody Court* is printed throughout in red ink. It is not only an early example of color printing, but a perfect example of harmony in text and type.

Another pamphlet from a secret press is probably the only extant example of a certain type of printing. It is, therefore, as uncommon as it is exotic. *Les Deux Conversations De M. de Neker* bearing the imprint

Geneva: Cruchaut, 1781, was printed by means of a brush, a primitive method that resulted in broken letters and uneven inking. The little octavo concerns the famous Madame Necker, salon leader and wife of Louis XVI's minister of finance. Her relations with a French writer, the Marquis de Pezay, are elaborated, her opinions on a free press discussed. The work is a kind of enigma involving the suggestion of scandal, a secret press, and printing by brush. To crown the attractions of our copy of *Les Deux Conversations* is its provenance. It bears the Goncourt monogram on both vellum covers, the Goncourt bookplate engraved by Gavarni, and the following ownership inscription: "Rarissime pamphlet imprimé à la brosse dans une imprimerie secrète. Il a été réimprimé en 1791. De Goncourt." Exotic? Assuredly. Uncommon? None more so.

The "excitingly strange" does not manifest itself with great frequency. From time to time it does appear—an alphabet to convert the heathen, an embossed typeface for the blind, the imprint of a printer who has led a double life, a trick book, a bloody pamphlet printed in bloody red, concrete typography in the sixteenth century, a diamond pendant on a title-page. Such samplings of the exotic, the uncommon, descend upon our desks like lightning flashes, falling stars that brighten the antiquarian world.

XII

Provenance

Abook has so many remarkable abilities. It instructs and it entertains; it extends horizons. Sometimes too it tells us its own history. Part of that history involves a variety of backgrounds and characters. Who owned the book? Through whose hands did it pass as it survived war and plague, suppression and upheaval? What experiences did it sustain? Was it cherished by bibliophiles? A source of knowledge, a fountain of ideas, did it sit supreme in a library or was it carried, perhaps in pocket edition, in the saddlebags of a bibliomaniac traveler? A study entitled *De La Bibliomanie* written in 1761 by Bollioud-Mermet, perpetual secretary of the Academy of Lyons, tells us much about collectors who found books irresistible and suffered the *manie de livres.*

During our decades in antiquarian books we too have encountered them—the bibliophiles whose prey was the printed page. Sometimes, like De Goncourt, they inscribed their books with telling remarks not to be found elsewhere. Sometimes they had them gloriously bound to treasure forever. We have met many of them on their travels and our own.

Not because they are the most important, but because they are the most likely owners of bookish treasures, we start with the royals. We shall continue with the lesser royals, and get on to the literary and the scholarly, as well as to the unknowns whose identity requires sleuthing—to the fascinating game of "Who owned what?"

Probably the highest royal who lodged temporarily on our shelves was Henry VIII of England. The thick octavo that had once been in his hands contained commentaries on Holy Writ by Haymo, Bishop of Halberstadt, whose moral and mystical musings, published in Cologne in 1529, probably had little effect upon the monarch. Its full calf binding, however, boasted two blind-tooled and stamped panels bearing the arms of Henry VIII and Catherine of Aragon mounted on both covers. The panels displayed the Tudor badges and Order of the Garter, and the center stampwork was enclosed by a motto: "Deus det nobis suam pacem et post mortem vitam eternam suam." At the time he acquired Bishop Haymo's commentaries, neither the peace of God nor the promise of eternal life was uppermost in Henry's thoughts. Although he was still married to Catherine of Aragon, his thoughts were rather on Anne

Boleyn, and papal sanction for the royal divorce had been demanded. Henry VIII himself was on the way to becoming the head of the English church when Bishop Haymo graced his library. As for the binding, we concluded that its two panels remained from the original full binding of the work. Henry had had a taste of the Bishop of Halberstadt, and we had a taste of Henry.

Henry's daughter by Anne Boleyn, Elizabeth I, would be a guest entertained by Thomas Wotton, and would offer him a knighthood. Though not a royal, he was in royal company. He was also a distinguished English bibliophile, dubbed "The English Grolier," a patron of learning, a collector of books "remarkable for their handsome bindings." One of them we bought abroad in October 1982: the great French scholar-printer Robert Estienne's dictionary of names, citing people and cities, rivers and mountains, idols and Biblical locations. Its binding of brown gilt calf had been made for Thomas Wotton. In the center of each cover was a medallion head showing Plato and Dido; on the front cover were the words: "Thome/Wottoni/Et Amicorvm 1548." On the back cover were the book's title and the owner's name. For the English Grolier and his Friends, here was a scholarly and beautiful Estienne. Thomas Wotton had an undeniably royal taste.

As a future Pope—the Pope who would develop the Vatican library—Felice Peretti, we felt, was also touched with nobility. When we found a copy of Pietro Vettori's commentaries of 1562 on the Greek orator Demetrius Phalereus bound for the future Sixtus V, we pounced upon it. Cased in black morocco, the gilt arms on both covers depicted an upright severed lion within a handsome gilt cartouche centered within a treble gilt border with fleurons in each corner. The title was stamped in gold on the front cover, and the book is stamped in gold in our memory.

Our royals and semi-royals continued to acquire books during succeeding centuries. Henry Howard, Earl of Northampton, son of the Earl of Surrey, was associated with the cause of Mary of Scotland and the revolt of Essex; he served on the council of James I. He also acquired books. One of them was highly appropriate for his shelves—*Le Tableav des Armoiries De France* by Philippes Moreau, a study of French heraldry published in 1609 that discussed marks of nobility and the reasons for coats of arms. Its calf binding was gilt-impressed on both covers with Howard's own coat of arms.

We were still more or less among the royals when we acquired the *Odes Sacrées* of 1758 by Pierre de Bologne, for the book bore on both covers the arms of Louis Philippe Duke of Orleans. Soldier, father of Egalité, grandfather of Louis Philippe King of the French, this Louis Philippe seems to have been a connoisseur of unusual reading matter. The *Odes* of Bologne, a lyric poet born in Martinique, included verses on a tempest in the American isles, on the Jews and their miseries in captivity, on earthquakes and floods. Louis Philippe's grandson would have been interested in it, for he had visited America and controlled a printing press during his years in Twickenham, long before he was elected King of the French.

A collector who was one of the greatest of the French Revolutionaries qualifies as a royal because he bore the title of Comte de Mirabeau. His arms were gilt-impressed on the binding of a charming romantic novelette that passed through our hands. The anonymous story entitled *Quelque Chose* had been published in The Hague in 1749 , the year Honoré Gabriel Riqueti, Comte de Mirabeau was born. Set in Spain, it must have provided escapist reading for him, and one wonders whether it might have been one of the books he was permitted when he was imprisoned in Vincennes. Did he scan it while he was writing his *Lettres de Cachet* in the blank leaves of books?

A few of our titled bibliophiles had American connections. Our 1735 edition of the *Mémoires* of the French marshal Villars carried the bookplate of Charles Cornwallis Ld Cornwallis. The record of the great military leader under Louis XIV would have been of enormous interest to Charles Cornwallis First Marquis and Second Earl Cornwallis, who surrendered at Yorktown on October 19, 1781. As the Cornwallis family copy, with the armorial bookplate bearing the family motto, the volume would have been at Charles Cornwallis' disposal. Perhaps it was with him at Yorktown!

Neither gilt-impressed on the cover nor carrying a bookplate, our first English translation of Voltaire's novel *Babouc*, published in London in 1754, did bear an ownership inscription on its flyleaf: "From the Earl of Moira's Library—Hastings." Francis Rawdon-Hastings, lst Marquis of Hastings and 2nd Earl of Moira, fought in the American Revolution, was adjutant-general to the forces in America, and remained in America from 1773 to 1781, the year of Cornwallis' surrender. Surely the two bibliophiles knew each other. Perhaps they swapped copies?

Our royal book owners included not only Henry VIII of England but Napoleon III of France. A French almanac we acquired in the early 1980s contained astronomical information, metric weights and measures, moneys, population statistics, and tables for the year 1863. This *Annuaire* published in Paris by the Bureau des Longitudes was bound in green morocco with gilt-impressed imperial arms and borders on both covers. It had been handsomely cased for the son of Louis Bonaparte King of Holland, Napoleon III. Charles Louis Napoleon Bonaparte had been given an excellent education and was well versed in engineering, history and science. He was also reactionary and despotic despite his democratic pretenses, and would be deeply involved in the tragic Mexican affair of Maximilian and Juarez. In 1863 perhaps he found relaxation as he turned the pages of our *Annuaire* whose binding carried his arms of stars and eagle surrounded by laurel wreath.

A non-royal who was truly royal ends our survey of high-and-mighty bibliophiles who have visited our premises. Unlike all the others, he flourished no title of nobility and hailed not from earlier centuries but from our own. His books—at least the two that we acquired—were neither handsomely bound nor in fine condition. They were as democratic as their owner. Their covers bore no gilt-impressed arms. They did not even boast a bookplate. But they were inscribed in the hand of our greatest twentieth-century president, Franklin Delano Roosevelt.

Some of Roosevelt's books, doubtless inadequately appreciated by his progeny, were sold at auction in the 1980s. From the heirs of one purchaser we happily and recently acquired two of them. Both had been acquisitions of Roosevelt's youth, and in all likelihood he had entered his inscriptions in them at the time of his recuperation from polio when he worked on his library. One was *The Pearl; or, Affection's Gift, For 1840. A Christmas and New Year's Present,* inscribed on the front endpaper and pastedown: "Franklin D. Roosevelt Hyde Park/Sartain plates." Below Roosevelt's signature were the words: "Miss A. Livingston from C.W. Halsted." *The Pearl* for 1840, with six plates including four by the eminent engraver John Sartain, had probably been given, as a Christmas or New Year's gift, to the boy Franklin by a relative in the Livingston family. Later, during his enforced leisure, he noted the fine "Sartain plates," a reflection of his interest in engraving.

Our other Roosevelt ownership inscription appeared in a copy of Nougaret's *Beautés De L'Histoire Des Etats-Unis de L'Amérique*

Septentrionale published in Paris in 1824. Its shabby front cover was gilt-stamped as a "Prix Pensionnat De Mr. Chastagner," and inscribed on the front free endpaper was the signature, "Franklin D. Roosevelt Hyde Park." This most appropriate addition to his library had doubtless been acquired during one of Roosevelt's many trips to France with his mother. A French survey of the United States, it unfolded the wonders of his country to the future president. What especially endeared the volume to us were the pressed leaves and flowers from the Hyde Park estate that had been scattered in its pages. Surely later, when he inscribed it, Roosevelt must have remembered his youth. For us it became a poignant reminder of the F.D.R. who was part of *our* youth—our non-royal who was truly royal.

While some royal ownerships are certainly indicative of royal interests, many—perhaps gifts of obsequious followers or sycophants—are not. When writers acquire books, on the other hand, their selections are more likely to be an index of their tastes. Literary provenances are generally more telling. They tell us not only what writers collected, but why, and what resulted from the ownership.

We have told some of those stories—those connections—in other collaborations about our holdings: the gift of Paracelsus' works to young Browning from his father, a gift that became a source for Browning's first great poem, *Paracelsus;* another most appropriate father's gift to a poet son, Tennyson's copy of Petrarch's poems; the copy of Tennyson's *Princess* that came into the possession of another Victorian giant, John Ruskin. Since those association copies passed from our hands, others have taken their place. They too tell stories of writers and the books they owned.

The great English patron of literature, the Earl of Chesterfield, placed his bookplate and shelf mark in what would become our copy of *La France Littéraire,* a dictionary of living French authors by Formey published in 1757. In the array of writers sketched, the Earl doubtless recognized many names and surely paused long over the account of his friend and correspondent, Voltaire. In *La France Littéraire* he had a useful literary dictionary.

On June 8, 1826, the romantic poet Robert Southey, friend of Wordsworth and brother-in-law of Coleridge, found himself in Antwerp. There he purchased a memento of his visit and inscribed it: "Robert Southey, Antwerp 8 June/ 1826." The book, by Gerard Goris, entitled *Les Délices de la Campagne A l'entour de la Ville de Leide,* was enriched with engraved title-page and twelve folding plates showing the chateaux of the different Flemish towns. The author's purchase was a vademecum of a journey, a souvenir for remembrance.

Another book designed to beguile travelers had an interesting Southey connection. In 1838, with the English poet and philanthropist John Kenyon, who introduced Robert Browning to Elizabeth Barrett, Southey made a tour through France. At Rouen they stopped long enough to purchase a book published in 1604, *Il Fvggilozio* by a Neapolitan writer Costo, who included stories and anecdotes, maxims and proverbs on jealousy and marriage, the malice of women and the neglect of husbands, tales to lighten tedious moments. It was Kenyon who entered the ownership inscription dated September 5, 1838: "In company with Robert Southey."

Another of England's great men of letters, the historian Thomas Carlyle, acquired a book from which perhaps he hoped to find diversion from sorrow. In 1867, Carlyle, in a state of complete depression after the loss of his wife, purchased the recently published life of Major-General James Wolfe by Robert Wright. The author of *The French Revolution* and *Frederick the Great* must have been fascinated by the life of the young English commander James Wolfe who led the army of the St. Lawrence and fell in 1759 on the Plains of Abraham in his great victory over the French. In his new acquisition, Carlyle penciled a few notes, pasted his "Humilitate" bookplate, and wrote his ownership inscription: "T. Carlyle Chelsea. Nov. 5, 1867."

As in the case of our Browning copy of Paracelsus, we had only one volume of Edward Wortley Montagu's *Genuine Memoirs* of 1781, but it bore on its title-page the ownership inscription of Robert Browning, a penciled note in his hand on page 29, and a bookticket: "From the Library of the late Robert Browning." The penciled note questioned a statement in the *Memoirs,* and read: "Edw. Wortley Montagu—born at Warncliffe lodge Yorkshire about 1714. If his father went to Constantinople as Ambassador 1716—the foregoing statement cannot be true." The statement Browning questioned concerned Montagu's birth. The *Genuine Memoirs* were anything but genuine. One of the gaffes it circulated was that the author and traveler Edward Wortley Montagu had been born in 1718, the illegitimate son of Lady Mary Wortley Montagu and the Grand Seignior of Turkey. Actually, Montagu had been taken to Constantinople by his parents in 1716 and there became the first British native inoculated for smallpox. Robert Browning was obviously well aware of the facts and of the memoirs' lack of authenticity.

More useful to its owner was a copy of the *Cento Novelle* of 1598 compiled by the Venetian savant Francesco Sansovino. This anthology of romances in prose and verse carried a notation inside its front cover: "Belonged to Dante Gabriel Rossetti & purchased at the sale of his books July 1882." The narratives in the collection, by Boccaccio, Bandello, Doni, and others, were enhanced by a series of delightful woodcuts, and the book was bound in gilt-stamped olive-green morocco. The illustrious pre-Raphaelite poet-painter Dante Gabriel Rossetti surely made good use of these Italian novelle in connection with his own work on *Early Italian Poets*.

Swinburne too was enchanted with things Italian. The author of "A Song of Italy" and "Siena" must have found much of interest in a collection of three orations on the Medici that bore the penciled note: "From Swinburne's Library Sale 19 June, 1916, lot 254." The Medici arms appeared on each title-page, and a portrait of Cosimo on one title verso. Swinburne's little collection, bound together in marbled limp boards, included eulogies of Cosimo I, Grand Duke of Tuscany, delivered in 1574 by Bandini, Angelio da Barga, and Vettori. The Italianate Englishman could immerse himself in them.

Across the sea too we pursue the owners and inscribers and givers of books, and garner a rich harvest from our findings. The provenances of American books make their own connections and yield their own stories of excitement for us to share.

Harvard, the oldest and most eminent American educational institution, appointed as its first incumbent of the Hancock Professorship of Hebrew, Stephen Sewall, the finest Hebraist of his time. In 1763 Sewall's *Hebrew Grammar*, designed for the use of Harvard students, was published in Boston—a book now rare since the Hebrew types used in its printing were destroyed by fire in January 1764. In our copy of Sewall's *Grammar* we found the author's ownership inscription as well as his textual annotations and emendations. We had Sewall's own copy of the first edition. It had apparently been passed on to his descendants, for it also bore the signatures of B. Sewall and Matilda Sewall. We passed it on to the precise place where it belonged—to Harvard University.

Very early in our firm's history, before Stern became Rostenberg's partner, Rostenberg found, among the discards moved from Columbia

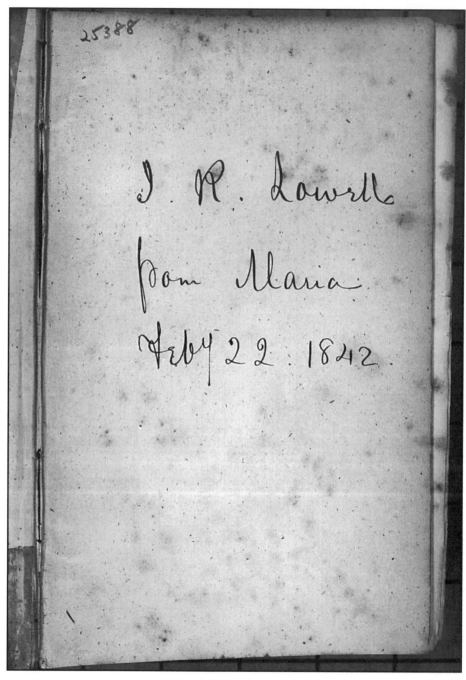

25388

J. R. Lowell
from Maria
Feby 22. 1842

Prelude to Marriage

University's library to the balcony of its bookstore, a copy of Elias Boudinot's *A Star in the West; or, a humble Attempt to discover the long lost Ten Tribes of Israel.* Boudinot, a distinguished jurist-statesman, attempted to prove that the American Indians were the original Ten Lost Tribes of Israel. His *Star in the West* was published in 1816, and the copy Rostenberg plucked from the shelves of the Columbia University Bookstore carried the following presentation inscriptions on the title-page: "Miss Edgeworth from her friend Mary Griffith. Charles H. Wharton the Gift of the Author." Maria Edgeworth, to whom the copy had been given by her friend Mary Griffith, was well-known as the author of children's stories and as the friend of Sir Walter Scott. Indeed she was perhaps better known than Charles H. Wharton who had received the copy from the author. Nonetheless, Charles H. Wharton is far more pertinently associated with this copy than Miss Edgeworth. At the time of publication in 1816, Boudinot was living in New Jersey where Wharton was a clergyman. More to the point—Charles H. Wharton had been named President of Columbia College! Now, in 1945, Leona Rostenberg found his copy of *A Star in the West* among the discards of Columbia University's library. By rights it should have been restored to Columbia. Instead it went to another appropriate library, that of the Hebrew University in Jerusalem.

In 1804, when Boudinot may have started interviewing Indians in his search for Israel's Lost Tribes, a young man named Daniel Webster was clerking in Boston for Christopher Gore. In between office sessions, on August 6, he picked up a book at a bookstore and paid $1.60 for it. We paid more when we purchased *Pursuits of Literature* by Thomas James Mathias. The book had been published in Philadelphia in 1800 for Joseph Nancrede of Boston, a Franco-American bookseller-publisher who helped American readers pursue the literature of France. Now we learned from his ownership signature that young Daniel Webster had also joined the pursuit of literature in 1804, the year before he began his practice at the bar.

The precise identity of a book's recipient cannot always be pin-pointed. We acquired during the 1980s a novel by the American writer and abolitionist Lydia Maria Child, *Philothea,* published in 1836. It carried a puzzling presentation inscription on its flyleaf: "To Mr. Richard Dana. With the respects of the Author." In this instance "Mr. Richard Dana" might have been Richard Henry Dana, Sr., poet, essayist, lecturer on Shakespeare, or his son Richard Henry Dana, Jr., author of *Two Years before the Mast.* If Mrs. Child had presented it to Junior, she may have done so upon the young sailor's return from the voyage that would be recreated in his classic story of the sea.

Lydia Maria Child was a friend of Margaret Fuller, whose Conversations on Boston's West Street she attended. Another member of Margaret Fuller's circle, the young transcendentalist Maria White, acquired a copy of a book that exerted a prime influence on the transcendental movement in America. Carlyle's *On Heroes, Hero-Worship, & The Heroic in History* appeared in first American edition in 1841 over the imprint of Appleton of New York. Our copy had an intriguing inscription: "J.R. Lowell from Maria Feby 22. 1842." Maria was Maria White, the future wife of the poet James Russell Lowell, described by him as "a glorious girl with the spirit eyes." They would be married on December 26, 1844.

A remarkable copy of Corneille's *Cid* published in Rome in 1727 went through a succession of provenances and carried us straight into the American twentieth century. Corneille's great tragi-comedy was translated into Italian as *Il Cid Drama per Musica* and adapted for performance at the Teatro Capranica in Rome in 1727. As French minister at Rome, Cardinal Melchior de Polignac doubtless witnessed the performance. Subsequently he had his copy of the *Cid* bound in an eighteenth-century French binding of burgundy morocco richly tooled in gilt with his arms on both covers. Still later the book acquired the booktickets of Walter Van Rensselaer Berry and Harry/Caresse. Walter Berry was none other than the inamorata of the great American novelist Edith Wharton, an impressive influence upon her life. Harry/Caresse carry us beyond Edith Wharton to F. Scott Fitzgerald, for Harry and Caresse Crosby were Fitzgerald's friends and patrons as well as founders of the Black Sun Press. Between the eighteenth century and the twentieth, these provenances trace a beguiling history.

The theatre seems to stimulate book mania. Sarah Siddons, probably the greatest English actress of all time, was the recipient of a book that she apparently treasured for years and left to her daughter. Compiled from original documents by the English dramatist and artist Prince Hoare, it was entitled *Memoirs of Granville Sharp* and published in London in 1820. It has an autograph inscription "Sarah Siddons" "From the Author." Since the author was a dramatist he must have been familiar with Sarah Siddons' interests, theatrical and non-theatrical. He must have been convinced that the first lady of the English theatre would profit from this work on the English philanthropist-reformer Granville Sharp who struggled to abolish the slave trade. Laid in the copy was a letter from Cecilia Siddons presenting it to Dr. Le Mann in June 1831. Perhaps Dr. Le Mann had attended the actress who died that year. When it came to us more than 150 years later, Cecilia's letter was still inside the book.

We had no copy of a book from Sarah Bernhardt's shelves, but we did have the catalogue of her library. The great French actress' books were sold in Paris on four summer days in 1923, the year of her death. The catalogue listed 750 works that reflected her taste and her scholarly attitude toward the stage. It included her repertory plays and works on the theatre, and among its highlights were five volumes of notices relating to La Bernhardt.

In the same way the auction catalogue of *Books from the Library of the Late David Belasco … Sold by Order of Mrs. Morris Gest* reflected the lifelong interests of the actor-dramatist-producer who died in 1931. This catalogue cited 185 items, among them numerous plays and inscribed books relating to the theatre as well as histories and background works for his own plays. The library was sold by order of Mrs. Morris Gest, daughter of David Belasco and wife of his distinguished young colleague Morris Gest.

It seems a natural corollary of their professional interests that women performers and women writers should collect books, but non-professional women also became notable book collectors and catalogues of their libraries provide keen insight into feminist learning. A single example each from France, England and America will indicate this.

A year after her death in 1736, the library of the Comtesse de Verrue was catalogued. Consisting of novels and plays, diplomacy and science, classics and Judaica, her collection was almost as varied as her life. The daughter of the Duc de Luynes, she married the Comte de Verrue and, against her wish, was forced to become the mistress of Victor Amadeus II, Duke of Savoy. She was poisoned, but somehow survived, escaped from Savoy, and became a salon leader and a book collector. Our copy of her library catalogue had been priced by hand. To complement it, we acquired an item from it, a collection of tragedies in a gilt calf binding bearing her armorial device along with the word "Meudon," site of her chateau.

Books from the library of a later English bibliophile appear from time to time on the market. Our copy of Senart's *Révélations... ou Mémoires,* an account of the atrocities committed during the Reign of Terror, bore the armorial bookplate of Frances Mary Richardson Currer, one of England's earliest collectors and a leading woman collector of Europe. Currer's library was sold by Sotheby in 1862, the year after her death, but we did not acquire her copy of Senart till 1997.

The bookticket of the distinguished California collector who was also a Countess of the Church, Estelle Doheny, was pasted in our copy of *The Seven Books ... against the Pagans* published in Cologne in 1536. Its author was the fourth-century Christian apologist Orosius, a disciple of St. Augustine, and his text is often described as a supplement to Augustine's *City of God.* This printed book had been converted into a work of art by the binder. The words "bound by John Reynes" strike joy in the heart of the lover of books, and certainly struck joy in "Countess" Doheny's heart. This sixteenth-century English binder had bound what would be her copy in brown calf over boards with central medallions of heads, surrounded by figurated border panels. The book deserved the binding it had been given, and there is no doubt that Estelle Doheny found its text as worshipful as its binding.

During the nineteenth century bibliographical recognition of women as scholars and book collectors had begun in earnest. One of the best examples that we researched was *Les Femmes Bibliophiles de France* (1886) by Bauchart. Here the French women bibliophiles of the sixteenth, seventeenth and eighteenth centuries are given their due. The work contains a numbered listing, with detailed bibliographical notes, of the manuscripts and printed books in various disciplines found in women's libraries. The bindings as well as a library interior are depicted on the full-page plates.

By the early twentieth century, a library of books by and about women was assembled by the New England minister and reformer, champion of anti-slavery, friend of woman, Thomas Wentworth Higginson, who proceeded to catalogue the collection. The only unfortunate part of his fine bibliographical study is the title he gave it—the Galatea Library. Galatea was shaped as a statue by Pygmalion who fell in love with his creation. Higginson's library was shaped by its writers, male and female, and although Higginson undoubtedly fell in love with it, he donated it to the Boston Public Library.

Multiple provenances of a single book often disclose connections between owners clearly and immediately, but sometimes the connections, if they exist, require sleuthing. No sleuthing was necessary to interpret the triple provenance of our copy of Helen Maria Williams' *Poems* published in two volumes in London in 1786. The verses of that English writer and translator who lived in France, supported the Revolution, and became part owner of the English Press in Paris, had been owned by the Shakespeare editor Isaac Reed. In 1807 when his library was auctioned in London, the two-volume set was purchased by the eminent collector Richard Heber; the third owner was the very distinguished bibliophile Sir Thomas Phillipps. That Helen Maria Williams had been in very prestigious hands required no detective work when we acquired her *Poems.*

More sleuthing was necessary when we tried to establish one or two ownerships by the great French bookseller-publisher-collector and bibliographer of the Aldine Press, Antoine Auguste Renouard. Bembo's history of the Venetian Republic published in Venice by that Press in 1551 was of interest to us on several counts. We invariably gravitated to Aldine imprints; in addition, Bembo's history contained an exciting bit of hidden Americana. Book 6 contained a reference to Christopher Columbus and his voyages and discoveries, describing him as "a man of sharp intellect, who traversed many immense regions and much of the ocean." The icing on the cake was the folio's bookticket. It read "Vigilantibus"—the motto of Archibald Acheson, 3rd Earl of Gosford. Sleuthing disclosed that in all likelihood the Gosford copy—our copy—had once been owned by the great Aldine bibliographer Renouard. Renouard's Aldine collection had been sold in 1828 to Samuel Butler, Bishop of Lichfield and Coventry, through the booksellers Payne and Foss. In 1839, when Butler died, his books were sold to that firm, and during the 1840s many of his Aldines were purchased by the 3rd Earl of Gosford. Our Bembo had almost certainly gone from Renouard to Butler to Gosford before it came to the sleuthing firm of Rostenberg & Stern.

Similar sleuthing convinced us that a little collection of three sixteenth-century Protestant works had also once been part of Renouard's library. The three anti-papal satires by Protestant reformers had been bound together in a gilt calf binding that bore on both covers the arms of the great collector Jacques Auguste de Thou and his wife Marie Barbançon. De Thou's copy had, we learned, eventually passed to the library of the Prince de Soubise, appearing as item 1709 in the 1788 catalogue of his library. Still later it passed to our friend, the distinguished Aldine bibliographer A.A. Renouard, appearing as item 2273 in his 1854 catalogue. More recently it appeared in the Rostenberg-Stern Catalogue 150 as item 80.

Close reading joined with intensive sleuthing to identify the owner of a London 1583 edition of Calvin's *Sermons*. The volume bore a lengthy and puzzling contemporary ownership inscription, reading:

"Mother my dewty to you premised &c. I will sende you this moste worthie worcke of Mr. Caluine for your Cart-wrighte & White-gifte. & I will praye you to sende me Bishop Alleys booke, for which if it please you you maye kepe the other Caluine upon Genesis. I desire you to sende Bishop Alleys booke by Nicle my Brother Erkenwalds man on Saturdaie nexte &c. March 11. 1592. Your Son at Comanndemt. John Wykes."

Rostenberg, author of several books on English printing history, tackled the problems: who was John Wykes?; who was Mother?; who was Bishop Alley?; who was brother Erkenwald?; who were Cart-wrighte and White-gifte? and came up with some guesses and more answers. The writer of the inscription was, she concluded, a cell member of an underground radical separatist religious group founded by Henry Barrow who was executed in 1593. Two of the books read by members were the work of Thomas Cartwright and John Whitgift, Archbishop of Canterbury. Alley was a bishop, author of *The poore man's librarie.* Erkenwald may have been of Dutch or German origin and may have traveled to England where he met with the Barrowists. As for Mother—the group included many women who were often addressed as Mother. In this case Mother was an extremely learned woman well read in Puritan literature. The connection between Calvin and the Barrowists needed no sleuthing, for the sect derived their ideology principally from the preaching of the Genevan reformer, author of *Commentaries Vpon Genesis* mentioned in the book's inscription. Rostenberg had sleuthed and come up with an exciting provenance; she had sleuthed not only the eleven lines of the inscription, but between the lines.

Sleuthing attempts do not always result in certainty or success. Sometimes they result in uncertainty and questions. Thomas Hollis was a staunch English Whig with as strong a passion for republicanism as for book collecting. He habitually had his books finely bound and often gave them away to his friends. Upon his death in 1774 he bequeathed to Harvard College 500 pounds for the purchase of books. We had two volumes that had been bound for Hollis: Locke's *Letters Concerning Toleration* in diced morocco with eagle resting on a quill gilt-impressed on the front cover. This the collector gave to the economist-dramatist William Shirley, as a penciled inscription indicates.

The recipient of our second Hollis remains doubtful, despite our sleuthing. Hollis himself had edited it before having it bound by the binder Matthewman in red morocco. It had been written originally by Henry Neville, author of *The Isle of Pines,* and entitled *Plato Redivivus Or A Dialogve Concerning Government.* There is no doubt that Hollis concurred with its message that, if England found stability, it would be a utopia, the greatest nation on earth. In this fourth edition of 1763 edited by Hollis we found a book stamp bearing the following words apparently in Hollis' hand: "Britannia/Victrix, Felix, Aeterna,/Pittoniana." We could interpret without any difficulty the first four words describing the land of hope and glory, but what about "Pittoniana"? We knew that Thomas Hollis' circle of friends included the great statesman and orator known now as the elder Pitt. Had Hollis given this copy of Neville's book to him? If so it would certainly have increased both its interest and its value. Is that what "Pittoniana" indicated? We were never able to determine this with any exactitude. In this case our sleuthing ended in a question mark.

However it ends, tracking down provenances is often one of the most rewarding of bookish adventures. The provenances of books purchased by writers on their travels, given to them by friends, dispersed in the sale of their libraries, bring us close to the owners. The owner, taking something from a book, also gives something to it. And we too, as temporary owners, transitory hosts, participate in this cycle of ownership in which the possessor becomes part of the possession.

Selected Short-Title Lists*

CHAPTER I: "WHAT'S PAST IS PROLOGUE"

BARTHOLINUS, Casparus. *De Aere Pestilenti corrigendo Consilium.* Copenhagen: Sartorius, 1619.

BEAUMONT, William. *Experiments and Observations on the Gastric Juice, and the Physiology of Digestion.* Plattsburgh: Allen, 1833.

CYRANO DE BERGERAC, Savinien. *Histoire Comiqve ... contenant Les Estats & Empires de la Lune.* Lyons: Fourmy, 1663.

DENIS, Jean Baptiste. "A Letter Concerning a new way of curing sundry diseases by Transfusion of Blood," *Philosophical Transactions of the Royal Society* No. 27 (22 July 1667).

EXPLANATION, An, of the Works of the Tunnel under the Thames from Rotherhithe to Wapping. London: Warrington, 1840.

[FIRMIN, Thomas]. *Some Proposals for the imploying of the Poor, Especially in and about the City of London. And for the prevention of Begging.* London: Aylmer, 1678.

HOWARD, Thomas. *On the Loss of Teeth and Loose Teeth; and on the Best Means of Restoring Them.* London: Simpkin & Marshall, 1861.

[LA FOLIE, Louis-Guillaume de]. *Le Philosophe Sans Prétention, ou L'Homme Rare.* Paris: Clousier, 1775.

LANGLEY, Samuel Pierpont. *Experiments in Aerodynamics.* Washington: Smithsonian Institution, 1891.

[MONTAGU, Lady Mary Wortley]. *Letters ... Written, during her Travels in Europe, Asia and Africa.* With [Montagu]. *An Additional Volume to the Letters.* London: Becket and De Hondt, 1763-1767.

PERSECUTION, La, Des Israélites en Russie. Paris: Marechal & Montorier, 1882.

[PIARRON DE CHAMOUSSET, Claude Humbert]. *Vues d'un Citoyen.* Paris: Lambert, 1757.

[PRUDHOMME, Louis-Marie]. *Histoire Générale et Impartiale des Erreurs, des Fautes et des Crimes Commis Pendant La Révolution Française.* Paris: Rue des Marais, 1797.

---

* Editions cited are not necessarily the earliest. They are those that have actually passed through our hands.

REPORT of the Committee for Investigating the Causes of the Alarming Increase of Juvenile Delinquency in the Metropolis. London: Dove, 1816.

RICHARDS, Ellen H. *The Chemistry of Cooking and Cleaning A Manual for Housekeepers.* Boston: Estes & Lauriat, 1882.

SAINTE-MARTHE, Scévole de. *La Manière de Nourrir Les Enfans à la Mammelle.* Paris: Luyne, 1698.

SIEGE de Paris. Lettre-Journal. Gazette des Absents. Paris: Jouast, 1870-1871. 40 issues.

[TIPHAIGNE DE LA ROCHE, Charles François]. *Giphantie.* Babylon 1760.

WELLS, William Charles. *An Essay on Dew.* London: Taylor & Hessey, 1814.

WITHERS, Thomas. *Observations on the Abuse of Medicine.* London: Johnson, 1775.

WOODMASON, James. *Proposals for Receiving Subscriptions, for an Apparatus By which Letters or other Writings may be copied at once.* [London 1780]. Broadside.

Suggested References

Bailey, James Osler. *Pilgrims through Space and Time.* New York: Argus, [1947].

Gove, Philip Babcock. *The Imaginary Voyage in Prose Fiction.* London: Holland Press, 1961.

McCulloch, John Ramsay. *The Literature of Political Economy.* London: London School of Economics, 1938.

Wolf, A. *A History of Science Technology, and Philosophy in the 16th & 17th Centuries.* London: Allen & Unwin, 1935. *...Eighteenth Century.* New York: Macmillan, 1939.

Chapter II: Eye-Witness Reports

ANTOMMARCHI, Francesco. *Mémoires ... ou Les Derniers Momens de Napoléon.* Paris: Barrois, 1825.

CARRA, Jean-Louis. *Mémoires Historiques et Authentiques sur le Bastille.* Paris & Maestricht 1789.

[CECIL, William, Lord Burghley]. *The Copie of a Letter Sent Ovt of England to Don Bernardin Mendoza Ambassadovr In France for the Kinge of Spaine, declaring the state of England.* London: Field, 1588.

CONFEDERATION Nationale Du 14 Juillet 1790. [Paris]: Sion, 1790.

HODGES, NATHANIEL. *Loimologia. Sive Pestis Nuperae apud Populum Londinensem Grassantis Narratio Historica.* London: Nevill, 1672.

[MARIE ANTOINETTE]. *Décret de la Convention Nationale du 3 Octobre 1793 ... Qui Ordonne le prompt Jugement de la veuve Capet au Tribunal révolutionnaire.* Paris: Imprimerie Nationale, 1793.

[MARY, QUEEN OF SCOTS]. *Mariae Stvartae Scotorvm Reginae, ... Svpplicivm & Mors.* Cologne: Kempense, 1587.

[MICHELANGELO BUONARROTI]. Eseqvie Del Divino Michelagnolo Bvonarroti Celebrate in Firenze dall' Accademia de Pittori, Scultori, & Architettori. Florence: Giunta, 1564.

[O'MEARA, Barry-Edward]. *Documens Particuliers (En Forme de Lettres) sur Napoléon Bonaparte.* Paris: Plancher, 1819.

SANDFORD, Francis. *The History of the Coronation of ... James II .... And of his Royal Consort Queen Mary: Solemnized in the Collegiate Church of St. Peter in the City of Westminster ... the 23 of April ... 1685.* Savoy: Newcomb, 1687.

TRUE, A, and Faithful Account of the Several Informations Exhibited To the Honourable Committee appointed by the Parliament to Inquire into the late Dreadful Burning of the City of London. [London] 1667.

[VICTORIA, Queen]. *The Tableau of the Procession at the Coronation of Queen Victoria, June 28, 1838; being An accurate Representation of that splendid Pageant.* London: Tyas, [1838].

Suggested References

Fletcher, Ifan Kyrle. *Splendid Occasions in English History 1520-1947.* London: Cassell, 1951.

Hohenemser, Paul. *Flugschriften-Sammlung Gustav Freytag.* Nieuwkoop: De Graaf, 1966.

Rostenberg, Leona. *Literary, Political, Scientific, Religious & Legal Publishing, Printing & Bookselling in England, 1551-1700: Twelve Studies.* New York: Franklin, 1965.

Chapter III: United Nations and Utopias

ALANTSEE, Ambrosius. *Tractatus qui intitulatur Fedus christianu[m].* Augsburg: Rinmann, 1504.

AUGUSTINE, Saint. *De la cita d'dio.* [Venice: Antonio di Bartolommeo, not after 1483]. 1st Italian edition; *Of the Citie of God.* [London]: Eld [for Thorp], 1610. 1st English edition.

CHARTER of the United Nations. New York: Volk, 1948.

DISSERTATION on the Subject of a Congress of Nations, for the adjustment of international disputes without recourse to arms. By A Friend of Peace. New York: Collier, 1837.

DUNANT, Jean-Henri. *Un Souvenir de Solferino.* Geneva: Fick, 1863.

ERASMUS, Desiderius. *Querela Pacis.* Paris: Colines, 1525.

GROTIUS, Hugo. *De Ivre Belli ac Pacis Libri Tres.* Paris: Buon, 1625.

[HALL, Joseph]. *Mvndvs Alter Et Idem.* Bound with BACON, Francis. *Nova Atlantis.* Bound with CAMPANELLA, Tommaso. *Civitas Solis Poetica.* Utrecht: Waesberg, 1643.

HARRINGTON, James. *The Oceana.* London 1700.

JAY, William. *War and Peace.* London: Ward, 1842.

KANT, Immanuel. *Zum ewigen Frieden.* Königsberg: Nicolovius, 1795.

MORE, Sir Thomas. *De Optimo Reip. Statv, Deqve noua insula Vtopia, libellus uere aureus.* Basle: Froben, November/December 1518.

ROUSSEAU, Jean-Jacques. *Extrait du Projet de Paix Perpétuelle de Monsieur L'Abbé de Saint-Pierre.* N.p. 1761.

ROUSSEAU, Jean-Jacques. *A Treatise on the Social Compact.* London: Becket & de Hondt, 1764.

SHAW, George Bernard. *The League of Nations.* London: Fabian Society, 1929.

SULLY, Maximilien de Béthune, Duke of. *Mémoires des Sages et Royalles Oeconomies D'Estat.* Amstelredam: Chez Aletinosgraphe, 1638.

Suggested References

Atkinson. Geoffroy. *The Extraordinary Voyaqe in French Literature.* Vol. I *Before 1700;* Vol. II *From 1700 to 1720.* New York: Franklin, n.d.

Beales, A.C.F. *The History of Peace: A Short Account of the Organised Movements for International Peace.* New York: Dial Press, 1931.

Figgis, John Neville. *Studies of Political Thought from Gerson to Grotius 1414-1625.* Cambridge: University Press, 1956.

Hearnshaw, Fossey John Cobb. *The Social & Political Ideas of Some Great French Thinkers of the Age of Reason.* New York: Barnes & Noble, [1950].

CHAPTER IV: HIDDEN AMERICANA

ACCOUNT, An, of the First Transatlantic Voyage of the Steam Ship Great Britain. Liverpool: Lace & Addison, 1845.

CHAPPEL, Samuel. *A Diamond or Rich Jewel, Presented to the Common-wealth of England, for the use of all Marchants and Tradesmen.* London: Clowes, 1650.

DAVIES, Samuel. *Religion and Patriotism The Constituents of a Good Soldier.* Philadelphia & London: Buckland, 1756.

DIVERSES Pièces Servans de Réponse Avx Discovrs Pvbliez Par Les Hollandois, svr ce qvi s'est passé entre l'Anqleterre et La Hollande. N.p. 1665.

HISTOIRE De la Dernière Guerre, Commençant l'An 1765 & finie par la paix d'Hubertsbourg le 15 Février 1763. Berlin 1767.

LOIS Des 26 & 31 Août 1792 … Qui Confére le titre de citoyens François à plusieurs Etrangers. Grenoble: Cuchet, [1792].

[MIRABEAU, Honoré Gabriel de Riqueti, Comte de]. *Avis Aux Hessois Et Autres Peuples de L'Allemagne Vendus par leurs Princes à l'Angleterre.* Cleves: Bertol, 1777.

[NEVILLE, Henry]? *Nvovo Scoprimento Dell' Isola Pines Situata oltre la linea Equinotiale.* Bolgna & Venice: Didini, [1668].

PSALTERIUM Hebreum, Grecum, Arabicum & Chaldeum, cum tribus latinis interpretationibus & glossis. Genoa: Porro, 1516.

RELATION D'Un Voyage du Pôle Arctique, au Pôle Antarctique, par Le Centre Du Monde. Amsterdam: Lucas, 1721.

SALA, George Augustus Henry. *The House That Paxton Built.* London: Ironbrace, Woodenhead & Co., 1851.

VECELLI, Cesare. *Habiti Antichi, Et Moderni di tutte il Mondo.* Venice: Sessa, 1598.

SUGGESTED REFERENCES

Age, The, of Exploration: An Exhibition Commemorating The Quincentennial of Christopher Columbus's First Voyage to the Americas. Provo: Friends of the Brigham Young University Library, 1992.

Chinard, Gilbert. *L'Amérique et la Rève Exotique dans La Littérature Française au xvii et au xviii Siècle.* Paris: Droz, 1934.

Faÿ, Bernard. *Bibliographie Critique Des Ouvrages Français Relatifs aux Etats-Unis (1770-1800).* New York: Franklin, 1968.

Italians, The, and The Creation of America. An Exhibition at the John Carter Brown Library Brown University prepared by Samuel J. Hough. Providence 1980.

CHAPTER V: CENSORSHIP AND SUPPRESSION

ARREST… Qui fait très-expresses inhibitions & défenses à tous Libraires & Imprimeurs faisant Profession de la R.P.R. de faire à l'avenir aucunes fonctions de Libraires & Imprimeurs. Paris: Leonard, 1685.

COMSTOCK, Anthony. *Traps for the Young.* New York: Funk & Wagnalls, 1883.

CONDEMNATIO Doctrinalis Martini Lvtheri per Qvosdam Magistros Nostros Lovanien et Colonien. Facta. N.p. ca. 1520.

DECREE, A, Of Starre-Chamber, Concerning Printing, Made the eleuenth day of July last past. 1637. London: Barker & Bill, 1637.

FIRST, The, and Large Petition of the City of London …: For a reformation in Church-Government, as also for the abolishment of Episcopacy. N.p. 1641.

JUDICIUM & Decretum Universitatis Oxoniensis … 1683. Contra Quosdam Perniciosos Libros. [Oxford]: Sheldonian Theatre, 1683.

LOVEJOY, Joseph C. and Owen. *Memoir of the Rev. Elijah P. Lovejoy. Who was Murdered in Defence of the Liberty of the Press.* New York: Taylor, 1838.

MILTON, John. *Areopagitica.* Hammersmith: Doves Press, 1907. [First Edition 1644].

MIRABEAU, Honoré Gabriel de Riqueti, Comte de. *Sur La Liberté De La Presse, Imité De L'Anglois, De Milton.* London 1788.

[PAINE, Thomas]. *The Genuine Trial of Thomas Paine, for A Libel contained in the second part of Rights of Man.* London: Jordan, 1793.

[PAUL IV, Pope]. *Index Avctorvm et Librorvm Qvi ab Officio Sanctae Rom … caveri ab omnibvs.* [Rome: Baldus, 1559].

PHILIP II, King of Spain. *Edictvm De Librorum prohibitorum Catalogo obseruando.* Bound with *INDEX Librorum prohibitorum.* Antwerp: Plantin, 1570.

PRYNNE, William. *Histrio-Mastix; The Players Scourge.* London: Sparke, 1633.

VOLTAIRE, François Marie Arouet de. *The History of the Misfortunes of John Calas, a Victim to Fanaticism.* Edinburgh: Williamson, 1776

VOLTAIRE, François Marie Arouet de. *Traité sur la Tolérance.* [Geneva] 1763.

WINTHROP, John. *A Short Story of the Rise, reign, and ruine of the Antinomians … that infested the Churches of New-England.* London: Smith, 1644.

[ZENGER, John Peter]. *The Trial of John Peter Zenger, Of New-York, Printer: Who was charged with having printed and published a Libel against the Government; and acquitted.* London: Almon, 1765.

SUGGESTED REFERENCES

Haight, Anne Lyon. *Banned Books.* New York: Bowker, 1955.

New York Public Library. *Censorship: 500 Years of Conflict.* New York: New York Public Library, 1984.

Reusch, Franz Heinrich. Indices librorum prohibitorum des sechzehnten Jahrhunderts. Tübingen 1886. *[Der Index der verbotenen Bücher].*

CHAPTER VI: STRATAGEMS OF SATAN

ACONZIO, Jacopo. *Stratagematvm Satanae.* Basle: Perna, 1565.

[AUBIN, Nicolas]. *Histoire des Diables de Loudun, Ou de la Possession des Religieuses Ursulines, Et de la condamnation … D'Urbain Grandier.* Amsterdam: Wolfgang, 1693.

CODRONCHIUS, Baptista. *De Morbis Veneficiis … Libri Qvattvor.* Venice: Senense, 1595.

DANEAU, Lambert. *Les Sorciers, Dialogve … povr ce temps.* [Geneva]: Bourgeois, 1574.

JAMES I, King of England. *Daemonologia.* Hanau: Antonius, 1604.

LE LOYER, Pierre. *IIII. Ljvres Des Spectres Ov Apparitions Et Visions D'Esprits.* Angers: Nepveu, 1586.

PICO DELLA MIRANDOLA, Giovanni Francesco. *Dialogus … Titulus est Strix, sive de Ludificatione Daemonum.* Bologna: Benedictis, 1523.

RECIT Véritable de ce qvi s'est passé A Lovdvn. Paris: Targa, 1634.

VIRET, Pierre. *Le Monde A L'Empire Et Le Monde Démoniacle.* Geneva: Laimarie, 1580.

WIER, Johann. *De Praestigiis Daemonum, & incantationibus ac veneficiis Libri sex.* Bound with WIER. *De Lamiis Liber.* Basle: Oporin, 1577.

SUGGESTED REFERENCES

Caillet, Albert Louis. *Manuel Bibliographique des Sciences Psychiques ou Occultes.* Paris: Dorbon, 1912.

Thorndike, Lynn. *A History of Magic and Experimental Science.* New York: Columbia University Press, 1941-1958. Vols. V–VIII.

CHAPTER VII: FEMINISM

AMERICAN, The, Spectator, or Matrimonial Preceptor. A Collection ... of Essays ... relating to the Married State ... adapted to the State of Society in the American Republic. Boston: Manning & Loring for West, 1797.

APPEAL, An, to the Women of the United States by the National Woman Suffrage and Educational Committee, Washington, D.C. Hartford: Case, Lockwood & Brainard, 1871.

[ASTELL, Mary/DRAKE, Judith]? An Essay In Defence of the Female Sex ... Written by a Lady. London: Roper and Wilkinson and Clavel, 1696.

COLONNA, Vittoria. Rime. [Venice: Salvionus], 1539.

DARDANO, Luigi. La Bella e Dotta Difesa delle Donne in Verso, e Prosa. Venice: Imperatore, 1554.

DISCOVRS Svr Le Divorce Qvi se Fait par L'Adultère, & si'l est permis à l'homme de se remarier. Par J.L.P.J.C.D. Paris: Richer, 1586.

[EON DE BEAUMONT]. [PEYRAUD DE BEAUSSOL]. La Vie Militaire, Politique et Privée de Demoiselle ... Eon ou D'Eon de Beaumont ... Par M. de la Fortelle. Paris: Lambert, 1779.

FULLER, Margaret. Woman in the Nineteenth Century. New York: Greeley & McElrath, 1845.

[GAUDEN, John]. A Discourse of Artificial Beauty, ...Between Two Ladies. London: Royston, 1662.

GOUGES, Marie-Olympe de. Séance Royale. Motion de Monseigneur Le Duc D'Orléans, ou Les Songes Patriotiques. N. p. 1789.

HROSWITHA, Opera. Wittenberg: Schroedter, 1707.

[JOAN OF ARC]. HORDAL, Jean. Heroinae Nobilissimae Ioannae Darc Lotharingae Vvlgo Avrelianensis Pvellae Historia. Pont-a-Mousson: Bernard, 1612.

[LE ROY, François]. Le liure de la femme forte et Vertueuse déclaratif du cantique de salomon es prouerbes. [Paris]: Petit, ca. 1505.

MARINELLA, Lucrezia. La Nobilta, Et L'Eccellenza delle Donne. Venice: Sanese, 1601.

MILL, John Stuart. The Subjection of Women. London: Longmans, Green, Reader, & Dyer, 1869.

[POULLAIN DE LA BARRE, François]. De L'Excellence Des Hommes, contre L'Egalité Des Sexes. Paris: Du Puis, 1675.

STAMPA, Gaspara. *Rime.* Venice: Pietrasanta, 1554.

STERN, Madeleine B. *We the Women: Career Firsts of Nineteenth-Century America.* New York: Schulte, 1962; Lincoln: University of Nebraska Press, 1994.

THOMAS (Antoine Léonard). *Essai sur Le Caractère, Les Moeurs Et L'Esprit Des Femmes Dans Les Différens Siècles.* Amsterdam: Harrevelt, 1772.

VIVES, Juan Luis. *De L'Vfficio del Marito, …De L'Istitvtione de la Femina Christiana.* Venice: Vaugris, 1546.

[WALSH, William]. *A Dialogue Concerning Women, Being a Defence Of the Sex.* London: Bentley, 1691.

[WILLIAMS, Helen Maria]. *A Residence in France, during the years 1792, 1793, 1794, and 1795; described in a series of letters from an English lady.* Elizabethtown: Kollock for Davis, 1798.

WOLLSTONECRAFT, Mary. *A Vindication of the Rights of Woman.* London: Johnson, 1792.

[WOODHULL, Victoria]. *Congressional Reports on Woman Suffrage. The Majority and Minority Reports of the Judiciary Committee of the House of Representatives on the Woodhull Memorial.* New York: Woodhull, Claflin & Co., 1871.

Suggested References

Anderson, Bonnie and Judith Zinsser. *A History of Their Own: Women in Europe from Pre-History to the Present.* New York: Harper and Row, 1988.

Kelso, Ruth. *The Doctrine of the English Gentleman in the Sixteenth Century, with a Bibliographical List of Treatises on the Gentleman and Related Subjects pubiished in Europe to 1625.* Urbana: University of Illinois Press, 1929.

Richards, Samuel Alfred. *Feminist Writers of the Seventeenth Century.* London: D Nutt, 1914.

Rostenberg, Leona and Madeleine Stern. *Between Boards: New Thoughts on Old Books.* Santa Monica: Modoc Press, 1989. Chapter 4: Feminism is Collectible, pp. 53-70, 184-191.

Ungherini, Aglauro. *Manuel de Bibliographie Biographique … des Femmes Célèbres.* Turin: Roux, 1892.

Chapter VIII: The Jews

ALPHABETUM Hebraicum Addito Samaritano Et Rabbinico. Rome: Congregation for the Propaganda of the Faith, 1771.

CONSIDERATIONS on the Bill to Permit Persons professing the Jewish Religion to be Naturalized by Parliament. Bound with *FURTHER Considerations on the Act to Permit Persons professing the Jewish Religion to be Naturalized by Parliament.* London: Baldwin, 1753.

GREGOIRE, Henri-Baptiste. *Essai sur la régénération physique, morale et politique des Juifs.* Metz: Devilly, 1789.

HERZL, Theodore. *Der Iudenstaat.* Warsaw 1896.

JOSEPHUS, Flavius. *Delle Antichita, e Guerre Giudaiche.* Venice: Milochi, 1682–1683.

KIMHI, David. *Commentarii … in Haggaeum, Zachariam & Malachiam.* Paris: Juvenis, 1557.

LEONE of Modena. *Cérémonies et Coustumes Qui s'observent aujourd'huy Parmy Les Juifs.* Paris: Billaine, 1674.

LOUIS XIII, King of France. *Lettres Patentes… à touts Iuifs & autres faisans profession & exercise de Iudaisme, de vuider le royaume, … à peine de la vie, & de confiscation de leurs biens.* Paris: Morel, Mettayer, 1615.

LUTHER, Martin. *Das Jhesus Christus ain geborner Jude sey.* [Augsburg: Raemminger, 1523].

MENASSEH BEN ISRAEL. [Hebrew title] *Hoc est, Spes Israelis.* Amsterdam: [Menasseh ben Israel], 1650. *The Hope of Israel.* London: Chapman, 1651.

MENDELSSOHN, Moses. *Jerusalem oder über religiöse Macht und Judentum.* Berlin: Maurer, 1783.

MIRABEAU, Honoré Gabriel de Riqueti, Comte de. *Sur Moses Mendelssohn, sur la Réforme Politique Des Juifs.* London 1787.

RECUEIL de Pièces Relatives A L'Admission des Juifs à L'Etat Civil. [Paris]: Lottin, [1790].

REUCHLIN, Johann. *Liber De Rvdimentis Hebraicis Liber Primvs.* Pforzheim: Anshelm, April 1506.

[VOLTAIRE]. [GUENEE, Antoine]. *Lettres de Quelques Juifs Portugais et Allemands, A M. de Voltaire.* Lisbon & Paris: Prault, 1769.

ZOLA, Emile. *Humanité—Verité—Justice. L'Affaire Dreyfus. Lettre A La Jeunesse.* Paris: Fasquelle, 1897.

SUGGESTED REFERENCES

Roth, Cecil. *A History of the Jews.* New York: Schocken, 1961.

Roth, Cecil. *The Jews in the Renaissance.* New York: Harper, 1959.

Steinschneider, Moritz. *Bibliographisches Handbuch über die ... literatur für hebraische sprachkunde.* Leipzig: Vogel, 1859.

CHAPTER IX: THE BLACKS

ADRESSE aux Nations de L'Europe sur Le Commerce Homicide appelé Traite des Noirs. London: Vogel, 1822.

ALMANAC Historique Nommé Le Messager Boiteux. Basle: Decker, 1791.

CLARKSON, Thomas. *An Essay on the Slavery and Commerce of the Human Species, Particularly The African.* London—Philadelphia: Crukshank, 1787.

CLARKSON, Thomas. *The History of the Rise, Progress, and Accomplishment of the Abolition of the African Slave-Trade by the British Parliament.* London: Longman, Hurst, Rees, and Orme, 1808.

CODE, Le, Noir, ou Recueil Des Règlemens rendus jusqu'à présent. Paris: Prault, 1767.

FAITS Relatifs à la Traite des Noirs. Paris: Crapelet, 1826.

[GILBERT, Olive]. *Narrative of Sojourner Truth, A Northern Slave, Emancipated ... by the State of New York, in 1828.* Boston: For the Author, 1850.

GRAYSON, William J. *The Hireling and the Slave, Chicora and other poems.* Charleston: McCarter, 1856.

GREGOIRE, Henri-Baptiste. *De La Littérature Des Nègres, ou Recherches sur leurs facultés intellectuelles, leurs qualités morales et leur littérature.* Paris: Maradan, 1808.

[LAVALLEE, Joseph]. *Le Nègre comme Il Y A Peu De Blancs.* Madras & Paris: Buisson, 1789.

MALOUET, Pierre-Victoire. *Mémoire sur L'Esclavage Des Nègres.* Neuchatel 1788.

[MAUPERTUIS, Pierre Louis Moreau de]. *Vénus Physique.* N.p. 1746.

MINUTES of the Evidence taken before a Committee of the House of Commons ... Relative to the State of the African Slave Trade. N.p. 1789-1790.

MOTT, Abigail Field. *Biographical Sketches and Interesting Anecdotes of Persons of Colour.* York: Alexander, 1826.

ORIGIN, The, of Jim Crow: Being An Authentic Account of the Life And Adventures of ... Jim Crow; ... By An American. London: Hodson, 1837.

TOCQUEVILLE, Alexis de. *Rapport ... relative aux Esclaves des colonies.* [Paris]: Henry, 1839.

[TOUSSAINT L'OUVERTURE]. DUBROCA, Jean François. *La Vie de Toussaint-Louverture, Chef des Noirs Insurgés De Saint-Domingue.* Paris: Dubroca & Bonneville, 1802.

[WELD, Theodore Dwight]. *American Slavery As It Is: Testimony of A Thousand Witnesses.* New York: American Anti-Slavery Society, 1839.

WHEATLEY, Phillis. *Poems on Various Subjects, Religious and Moral.* London: Bell, 1773.

SUGGESTED REFERENCES

Johnson, Charles, Patricia Smith and the WGBH Series Research Team. *Africans in America: America's Journey through Slavery.* New York: Harcourt Brace, 1998.

Schomburg, Arthur Alfonso. A Bibliographical Checklist of American Negro Poetry. New York: C. F. Heartman, 1916.

CHAPTER X: THE LURE OF FIRSTS

CELLINI, Benvenuto. *Vita.* Cologne [Naples]: Martel, [1728] .

CONSTITUTIONS des Treize Etats-Unis de L'Amérique. Philadelphia & Paris: Pierres—Pissot, 1783.

COOPER, William. *A Catalogue of Chymicall Books.* London: [Cooper], 1675.

[FRANKLIN]. [WOLLASTON, William]. *The Religion of Nature Delineated.* London: Palmer, 1725.

GERSAINT, Edmé François. *Catalogue Raisonné De Toutes Les Pièces Qui forment l'Oeuvre De Rembrandt.* Paris: Hochereau, 1751.

GODWIN, William. *Enquiry concerning Political Justice, and Its Influence on Morals and Happiness.* Philadelphia: Bioren & Madan, 1796.

JOHNSON, Samuel. *A Dictionary of The English Language.* Philadelphia: Moses Thomas, 1818.

MONTESQUIEU, Charles de Secondat. *The Spirit of Laws.* Worcester: Isaiah Thomas, Jun., 1802.

MOZART, Leopold. *Gründliche Violinschule.* Augsburg: Lotter, 1770.

NANCREDE, Joseph. *L'Abeille Françoise, ou Nouveau Recueil, De Morceaux Brillans, Des Auteurs François Les Plus Célèbres.* Boston: Belknap et Young, 1792.

ROUSSEAU, Jean-Jacques. *Du Contrat Social, ou Principes Du Droit Politique.* Paris: Defer de Maisonneuve, 1790.

WYTFLIET, Cornelius. *Histoire Vniverselle Des Indes Occidentales Et Orientales, et de la Conversion des Indiens.* Douai: Fabri, 1611.

SUGGESTED REFERENCES

Hirschberg, Leopold. *Der Taschengödeke Bibliographie deutsches Erstausgaben.* Munich: Deutscher Taschenbuch Verlag, 1970.

Parenti, Marino. *Prime Edizioni Italiane.* Milan: Libri d'Arte e di Filologia, 1948.

Stern, Madeleine B., "Some French Revolutionary Imprints: Patterns from the past," *Bulletin du Bibliophile* (1991).

Tchemerzine, Avenir. *Bibliographie d'Editions Originales ... d'Auteurs Français* des XVe, XVIe, XVIIe et XVIIIe siècles. Paris: Plée, 1927-1934.

CHAPTER XI: THE PRESS: EXOTIC AND UNCOMMON

[BALZAC, Honoré de]. DUPIN, André-Marie-Jean-Jacques. *La Liberté Individuelle, ou Plaidoyer et Réplique.* Paris: Baudouin—Balzac, 1826.

BOISSAT, Pierre. *Le Brillant de la Royne, ov Les Vies des Hommes Illustres du nom de Médicis.* Lyons: Bernard, 1613.

CASTIGLIONE, Bonaventura. *Gallorvm Insvbrvm Antiqvae Sedes.* Milan: Castiglione, 1541.

[CERCLE SOCIAL]. *Imprimerie Et Librairie Du Cercle Social, Rue du Théatre-Français, No. 4.* [Paris]: Imprimerie du Cercle Social, ca. 1793?

CONGREGATIO PROPAGANDAE FIDEI. Type spcimens of exotic alphabets issued by the Press of the Congregatio. Rome 1629—1784.

GUILLIE, Sébastien. *Essai Sur L'Instruction des Aveugles.* Paris: Imprimé par les Aveugles, 1817.

MOON, William. *Light For The Blind.* London: Longmans, 1873.

REMERCIMENT Des Imprimevrs A Monseignevr Le Cardinal Mazarin. Paris: Boisset, 1649.

SUGGESTED REFERENCES

Bigmore, E.C. and Wyman, C.W.H. *A Bibliography of Printing.* New York: Duschnes, 1945.

Updike, Daniel Berkeley. *Printing Types: Their History, Forms and Use A Study in Survivals.* Cambridge: Harvard University Press, 1937.

CHAPTER XII: PROVENANCE

BAUCHART, Ernest Quentin. *Les Femmes Bibliophiles de France (XVIe, XVIIe, & XVIIIe Siècles)*. Paris: Morgand, 1886.

[BELASCO, David]. *Books from the Library of the Late David Belasco. ... Sold by Order of Mrs. Morris Gest*. New York: American Art Association Anderson Galleries, 1931.

[BERNHARDT, Sarah]. *Bibliothèque de Mme Sarah Bernhardt*. Paris: Leclerc-Giraud-Badin, 1923.

[BROWNING, Robert]. MONTAGU, Edward Wortley. *Genuine Memoirs*. London 1781.

[CARLYLE, Thomas]. WRIGHT, Robert. *The Life of Major-General James Wolfe*. London: Chapman & Hall, 1864.

[CHESTERFIELD, Philip Dormer Stanhope, 4th Earl of]. FORMEY, Jean Henri Samuel. *La France Littéraire, ou Dictionnaire des Auteurs François Vivans*. Berlin: Haude & Spener, 1757.

[CURRER, Frances Mary Richardson]. SENART, Gabriel-Jérome Senar. *Révélations puisées Dans Les Cartons Des Comités de salut public et de sureté générale; ou Mémoires (Inédits) de Senart*. Paris: Les Principaux Libraires de France, 1824.

[DE THOU, Jacques Auguste]. CURIO, Coelius Secundus. *Pasqvillvs Ecstaticvs*. [Basle ca. 1565]. Bound with *BVLLA Diaboli*. ca. 1555. Bound with [FLACIUS Illyricus, Mathias]. *Epistola de Morte Paul Tertij. Pot. Max.* [Piacenza] 1549.

[DOHENY, Estelle]. OROSIUS, Paulus. *Adversvs Paganos ... Historiarvm Libri Septem*. Cologne: Hittorp, 1536.

[HENRY VIII, King of England]. HAYMO, Bishop of Halberstadt. *In XII. prophetas minores enarratio*. Cologne: Cervicorn, August 1529.

[HOLLIS. Thomas]. NEVILLE, Henry. *Plato Redivivus, or A Dialogue Concerning Government*. London: Millar, 1763.

[LOWELL, James Russell]. CARLYLE, Thomas. *On Heroes, Hero-Worship, & The Heroic in History*. New York: Appleton, 1841.

[MIRABEAU, Honoré Gabriel de Riqueti, Comte de]. Anon. *Quelque Chose*. The Hague: Neaulme, 1749.

[NAPOLEON III, Emperor of the French]. Anon. *Annuaire Pour L'An 1863*. Paris: Mallet-Bachelier, [1863].

[ROOSEVELT, Franklin Delano]. NOUGARET, Pierre Jean Baptiste. *Beautés De L'Histoire Des Etats-Unis de L'Amérique Septentrionale.* Paris: Brunot-Labbé, 1824.

[ROOSEVELT, Franklin Delano]. Anon. *The Pearl; or, Affection's Gift, For 1840. A Christmas and New Year's Present.* Philadelphia: Anners, [1839].

[VERRUE, Jeanne-Baptiste d'Albert de Luynes, Comtesse de]. *Cataloque Des Livres De Feue Madame La Comtesse De Verrue.* Paris: Martin, 1737.

[WEBSTER, Daniel]. [MATHIAS, Thomas James]. *Pursuits of Literature.* Philadelphia: Maxwell for J. Nancrede, Boston; and Dickins and Ormrod, Philadelphia, 1800.

[WOTTON, Thomas]. [ESTIENNE, Robert]. *Hebraea, Chaldaea, Graeca et Latina Nomina virorum, mulierum, populorum ... quae in Bibliis leguntur, restituta.* Paris: Robert Estienne, 1537.

SUGGESTED REFERENCES

Bonnaffe, Edmond. *Dictionnaire des Amateurs français au XVIIe Siècle.* New York: Franklin, n.d.

De Ricci, Seymour. *English Collectors of Books & Manuscripts (1530-1930) and Their Marks of Ownership.* Bloomington: Indiana University Press, 1960.

Fletcher, William Younger. *English Book Collectors.* London: Kegan Paul, Trench, Trübner, 1902.

Index